MW00473009

UNTOUCHABLES

Honest Conversations About Subjects
We Would Rather Not Discuss

Jack Hilligoss

Sermon To Book
www.sermontobook.com

Untouchables / Jack Hilligoss
ISBN-13: 9780692482087
ISBN-10: 0692482083

To Jenelle, my best friend, cheerleader, and wife. You are the best gift God ever gave me.

CONTENTS

Absolute Truth 3

Pure Religion 19

Heaven and Hell 39

Miracles... 55

Repentance 71

Holiness... 87

Sexual Purity 103

Generosity 119

The Race Card.. 131

Gay Marriage 143

Politics... 153

About The Author 166

About Sermon To Book 168

CHAPTER ONE

Absolute Truth

To the Jews who had believed him, Jesus said, "If you hold to my teaching, you are really my disciples. Then you will know the truth, and the truth will set you free." They answered him, "We are Abraham's descendants and have never been slaves of anyone. How can you say that we shall be set free?" Jesus replied, "Very truly I tell you, everyone who sins is a slave to sin. Now a slave has no permanent place in the family, but a son belongs to it forever. So if the Son sets you free, you will be free indeed." **(John 8:31-36 NIV)**

Jesus is in a debate.

I use the word "debate" because it is a much nicer, more Jesusy word than "argument" or "fight."

So, Jesus is in a debate. And the debate is about truth.

Not mathematical truth like 2 + 2 = 4. Not historical truth like the fact that George Washington was the first president of the United States. But truth that is just as true and infinitely more important than any other truth. Truth that gives meaning and importance to all the other things we call true.

Truth about right and wrong. About morals. About loving God and others, and how we ought to live our lives. Without that truth, everything else we learn from kindergarten to graduate school constitutes uninspiring facts.

Jesus made the Jews he was debating with angry. People tend to get angry in debates over these sorts of things. The difference is that these men knew why they were ticked off. They believed that they were right and he was wrong. Jesus's angers us also, we just don't understand why.

An Unseen Influence

I moved from the Midwest to Florida in the month of January.

Pure genius!

In January, it was impossible for me to understand why everyone from the Midwest had not followed me to this breezy, sunny, tropical paradise.

Then June showed up.

In the month of June, Florida jumps on your chest with two hot, stinky feet and introduces you to his little friend: *humidity*. Humidity greets you with a moist, warm hug every morning and hangs around you all day.

You cannot see, taste, or touch humidity, but it is there all the time. It is a factor in the when, where, what, and why of all your decisions. Humidity has incredible influence.

In the same way, we live in a culture that is saturated with an idea.

You cannot see, taste, or touch it, but it is in the atmosphere all around us. It is in the music we download, the movies we watch, and the curricula we study in school.

It is *relativism*—the philosophy that absolute truth, which is the sort of truth Jesus asserted, does not exist; or if it does, it is not knowable. We all have been influenced by that idea in some way.

People look at you as if you are some sort of flat-footed Philistine if you stomp around in their coffeehouse conversations talking about truth. But here are some uncomfortable facts:

Jesus claims there is truth and says He knows that truth. Jesus makes it clear that there are such things as right and wrong. There are moral and spiritual precepts that are "true" and "false." There are beliefs that uplift and empower and others that will debase and degrade us. There are teachings that are good and there are teachings that are evil.

Jesus imposes His truth upon us. *"If you continue in my teaching, you will know the truth…"* We may have been willing to indulge Jesus when He asserted that truth existed. We can smile benignly and indulge that harmless delusion with a patronizing sentiment like "to each his own." But now Jesus is trying to impose His idea of truth on us. That is absolutely over the line! Not only is that socially repugnant, it is also politically incorrect. Jesus will never keep a job, land a promotion, or gain tenure talking like that.

Jesus tells us we can know the truth. It may be repugnant to our culture to hear Jesus say that He knows the truth. However, most of us who profess to be Christians will concede that point readily. But Jesus ratchets up the heat on us when He says, *"You will know the truth..."*

This makes it clear that truth is accessible to us. Ignorance will never be an excuse for our failure to live according to truth. Knowing objective truth may be a matter of intellect and education, but knowing how we should live is a matter of desire and will.

Finally, Jesus tells us that it is possible for us to live the truth. He makes it clear that we are expected to hold to His teaching. Jesus never taught moral theories. He taught moral realities and moral imperatives. He expected us to hold to His teaching.

Pause for a moment and reflect with me on that radical idea. Think about some of the things Jesus tells us to do:

- Forgive people who sin against you "seventy times seven times."

- If someone slaps you on one cheek, give them a shot at the other.

- Bless people who curse you, pray for people who persecute you, and do good to those who use you.

How are you doing so far? Are you uncomfortable? Defensive? Angry?

No matter what our initial reaction, our response needs to be an attempt to deal honestly with the implications His words have for our lives.

For instance…

Truth Exists

I think I mentioned that Jesus was in a debate.

A debate requires two sides. Every human being has an idea about "truth." Every one of us innately believes there is a moral and spiritual absolute that should govern our behaviors. We all believe in right and wrong. These ideas are not outdated relics. They are woven into the fabric of our hearts.

Tim Keller, Pastor of Redeemer Presbyterian Church in Manhattan, wrote about a young couple who came to speak with him about officiating their wedding.

They wanted a church wedding and a traditional ceremony. Not because they were churchgoers or held to scriptural teachings, but because they were sentimental and their parents felt it was important.

Keller was curious why they did not share their parents' faith. The young lady made it clear that she was repulsed by the dogmatic stance the church took on many moral issues.

Keller asked her, "Do me a favor. Tell me something that you think is wrong."

"I think mistreatment of women is wrong," she responded.

Keller agreed, "I feel the mistreatment of women is wrong because the Scriptures teach that God made human beings with equal value and worth, so we ought to treat each other with dignity because we were made in the image of God." Then he prodded, "Why do you think it's wrong?"

She didn't hesitate. "Everyone knows it's wrong to violate the rights of another person."

"Actually," Keller gently corrected, "many cultures in the world don't think that way at all. They do not believe it's wrong to mistreat women. The fact is most of the people in the world don't share your view of human rights at all." He went on, "If I were to say to you, 'All women are inferior to men,' you'd get angry and respond, 'That is not an argument, that is just an assertion'—and you would be right. So let's start again. If there is no God, and no one can really say there are moral absolutes—why is it wrong to trample on another person's rights?"

She sat silently for a second, shrugged, and answered, "I don't know, I guess I just feel that it is wrong."

We hear it over and over in our world: Everyone should be free to pursue and live their own values. No one has the right to impose his or her idea of morality on anyone else.

The problem is, we all have an innate sense of truth, and we all try to impose our truth on others. In fact, when you tell someone they shouldn't try to impose their values on others, you are imposing your values on them!

We can't help ourselves; we are wired this way because that is the nature of the One who created us.

If you think that everyone in America should have access to free, government-funded healthcare and you vote to make that happen, you are attempting to impose your morality on the rest of the country. If you believe that gay marriage should be a civil right and that businesses should be penalized for not recognizing that right, you are imposing your values on those who disagree with you.

We all do it. Jesus did it, Pharisees did it, Democrats do it, Republicans do it, gay activists do it, Independent Fundamentalists do it, Baptists do it. We all operate from a belief that right and wrong exist and that it is good for all humanity to live in line with what is right and true.

Maybe I can make this simpler. Suppose we are eating lunch together and you order a sandwich that I like, and I decide that I am either tougher or, more likely, faster than you are, so I steal your sandwich.

If, as you chase after me, you yell, "Hey! That's mine! You shouldn't have taken it!" then in that moment, you have just confessed that there is an absolute truth.

Truth Is Crucial

Jesus's teaching shows us what Dallas Willard called "the power of mere ideas."

Whenever I hear the dismissive statement, "It doesn't matter what you believe as long as you believe it sincerely enough," I react like a mother watching a toddler play in the street.

Beliefs are the most powerful factor in human life. Our ideas about what is good and right actually shape our lives. We make decisions and take actions based upon them. Those actions have real consequences.

Jesus says we can *"know the truth"* and be set free, or we can ignore truth and become a slave to sin (John 8:32, 34).

Emerson said it this way: "Sow a thought and you reap an action; sow an act and you reap a habit; sow a habit and you reap a character; sow a character and you reap a destiny."

The Scriptures are much more direct: *"For as he thinks in his heart, so is he."* (Proverbs 23:7 NKJV).

Saying, "It doesn't matter what you believe as long as you are sincere about it," is lazy at best. However, more often that approach to truth is deadly.

Sincerity Cannot Be the Test of Truth

We are capable of believing things sincerely that lead to actions that are destructive to others and ourselves.

Hitler was full of passionate sincerity when he exterminated six million Jewish people and mangled the world with a war. ISIS is full of delusional sincerity when they raid villages, murder, torture, and rape.

I could climb to the fourteenth floor of the Grand Hotel in my hometown with the sincere belief that I can fly.

But I would be sincerely wrong. And if I take a leap based upon that belief, I will be sincerely dead.

Truth is truth. If we live in denial of truth, the result will be destructive. However, truth by its nature is given to us for our good.

Which leads to this implication…

Jesus's Truth Makes Real Freedom Possible

"If you hold to my teaching…Then, you will know the truth, and the truth will set you free." **(John 8:31-32 NIV)**

Well, what does it mean to be free?

If I were to conduct a man-on-the-street interview and ask that question of one hundred people, ninety-nine would offer some variation of this response: "Freedom is being able to do whatever I want to do whenever I want to do it."

Our idea of freedom is the absence of any rules, boundaries, or restrictions on our choices and behaviors. But Jesus says that freedom is experienced when we hold to His teachings.

"Wait a minute," I hear the protest, "doing what someone else tells me to do isn't freedom!"

That's the point! Pay attention to how Jesus responds to the protest:

"So if the Son sets you free, you will be free indeed" (John 8:36 NIV).

Really free. Not living with a false illusion of freedom the world sold you and you bought into.

You see…

We don't understand freedom. The problem with our concept of freedom is simple: it doesn't exist!

We have never really understood freedom, have we? We have always had such an amazing capacity to live in denial.

The Jews respond to Jesus, *"We are Abraham's descendants and have never been slaves to anyone. How can you say that we shall be set free?"* (John 8:33 NIV).

Never been slaves? Ever heard of Egypt? Four hundred or so years in slavery! Read the book of Judges! They were in slavery in that one period to the Philistines, the Amorites, the Hittites, and a few other "-ites." Then there was Babylon, Medio-Persia, and Greece. By the way, you are in slavery to Rome right now!

But I digress. Jesus doesn't.

He doesn't take the time to slap down the obvious political denial. Rather, he moves to the area that is more critical and where we exercise even greater denial:

"Very truly I tell you, everyone who sins is a slave to sin" (John 8:34 NIV).

Real freedom and bondage are heart issues, and this is where we engage in our greatest self-deception.

While there is such a thing as absolute truth, there is no such thing as "absolute freedom." We were created with the freedom to make choices. But we are not free to control the outcome of those choices. And every moral choice has a lasting impact on our spirit.

Jesus tells us we are either free or a slave, and the determining factors are the decisions we make in regard to His truth.

Will we submit to His truth or insist on living our own way?

You say you are free and nothing controls you because you live in the good old USA. But Jesus understood that there is a kind of jailer who handcuffs and imprisons us.

Whatever you want to quit and can't—that's your owner! Whatever you know is real bad for you but it is so good to you that you cannot leave it alone, that's your jailer! If it is greater than your will and stronger than your desire to be holy—that's your master. If you can't function without drinking it, smoking it, or powering it up, then you are not free.

If you let people use you sexually because you are afraid of being alone, that's your jailer.

If you are working ungodly hours to keep up with three car payments and two mortgages and you cannot afford to give even a small percentage of your income to others, then that's your master

If I could say a name and thoughts of jealousy and revenge rise up like Pavlov's dogs in you, then you are a slave.

And all that shows us:

Freedom means more than we ever imagined.

Brennan Manning related a story of a young lady who had lived an alcoholic and promiscuous life but who began to show up at a Bible study he was leading. After one session, she approached him hesitantly and asked, "Do you mean that God's grace makes me able to not do everything I want to do?"

Exactly!

That is the freedom Christ's grace and truth makes possible. That is the freedom we need so desperately.

Romans 6:19 says, *"I am speaking in human terms, because of your natural limitations. For just as you once presented your members as salves to impurity and to lawlessness leading to more lawlessness, so now present your members as salves to righteousness leading to sanctification"* (ESV).

Whatever we submit to, its control and power over us will be ever-increasing. So freedom is not being able to do whatever I want; freedom is the God-given power to do what is right and good. And Jesus says that happens when we live according to His truth. Now, let us be sure to understand…

A Critical Caveat

I am fascinated by the circumstances that led up to this debate between Jesus and the Jews. It really began because the Jews were trying to come to grips with the radical claims Christ was making about Himself.

Then something amazing happens: *"Even as he spoke, many believed in him"* (John 8:30).

That is awesome! That is what it is all about! Getting people to make professions of belief in Jesus is what we live for in Christendom.

It is why we have the bonfire and sing-along with guitars at the end of every youth camp.

It is why we hold those huge, international, high-octane, Jesus-is-the-coolest worship fests.

It is all for that moment when, with every head bowed and every eye closed, we can have people come to altars, or fill out decision cards, and tell them they are now Christians.

Forgiven, free, saved, for sure—forever.

But Jesus doesn't do any of those things.

"To the Jews who had believed him, Jesus said, 'If you hold to my teaching, you are really my disciples. Then you will know the truth, and the truth will set you free'" (John 8:31–32 NIV).

Something in our evangelical hearts wants to interrupt: "Jesus, they prayed the prayer, they signed the card, we gave them the T-shirt. They already made the decision."

The thing is, Jesus wasn't after decisions; He was after disciples. And the promise of freedom is given to disciples—not those who profess, but those who live the truth.

One saint said it this way: "The faith is not yours until you live it."

And let's face it, the church is full of people who believe all the orthodox teaching *about* Jesus, but they do not do what Jesus told them to do.

So we don't know the truth, and it hasn't set us free. We are just as addicted, just as controlled by lust, just as filled with bitterness, just as dominated by debt and consumerism, just as miserable in marriage as people who have no faith in Jesus. We are alienated from the life He said we could have even though we believe in Him.

We have begged Him for forgiveness for the life we have lived, but we have not made a commitment to build our new lives on His truth.

Jesus says that we will be free when we know the truth. The word "know" is a word describing intimate friendship or knowledge gained through relationship and experience.

Many have a technical, orthodox, Sunday-school knowledge of Jesus. That is the level of our belief and understanding. But we have never experienced life as He describes it. We have never known truth and the freedom He said would come through that truth.

Thankfully, Jesus offers us a wonderful ray of hope...

The Miraculous Gift of Freedom

"Now a slave has no permanent place in the family, but a son belongs to it forever. So if the Son sets you free, you will be free indeed" (John 8:35–36 NIV).

Jesus knew His antagonists were bluffing. Religious people are very good at bluffing—at trying to convince others and themselves that they are more certain, more sure, and better in every way than they really are.

"We are Abraham's descendants," they shout.

And we join the chorus, "We are Baptists!"

"We have been good Presbyterians all our lives!"

"Why, I had an ecstatic experience and spoke in tongues once!"

We are trying to shout down the annoying whisper of the slave that still lives in our hearts.

We haven't really been set free; we haven't really ever experienced the touch of God's grace—so we are religious slaves. Frightened to death that we could be found out and sold out at any given time!

Being a descendent of Abraham doesn't free you. Being confirmed or dedicated doesn't do that for you. Being a Baptist or a Presbyterian or a Pentecostal doesn't do that for you.

"If the Son sets you free, you will be free indeed!"

Truth is a schoolmaster who makes us realize that only Jesus can empower us to continue in His words and experience His freedom.

It isn't easy. But, through the grace of Christ, it is possible.

CHAPTER TWO

Pure Religion

Religion that God our Father accepts as pure and faultless is this: to look after orphans and widows in their distress and to keep oneself from being polluted by the world.
(James 1:27 NIV)

The Mall at Millenia was packed.

My wife and I, and dozens of other desperate diners, were waiting to have our names called in the Cheesecake Factory seating lottery.

The far too young and chipper receptionist told us it would be about forty-five minutes. So we decided to take a stroll around the cavernous shopping center.

That is when I saw a store named True Religion. How can a preacher pass up any place that is offering that?

In we went…

It turns out True Religion is a chain of stores that sells blue jeans and all sorts of denim accessories. They definitely have zeal for their product.

Their website includes a page entitled "The True Story: The stitch that started it all." That page details its "five needle thread at two stitch per inch process" using phrases like "Super T Stitch," "Be So Bold Attitude," and "designed by the fearless for the fearless."

Hallelujah!

I wanted True Religion! Until I looked at the price tag and saw that they wanted over $200 for their jeans! I decided True Religion cost too much. I'll stick with my Levi's.

Whenever True Religion is too costly, everyone looks for a cheap knock-off. And when it comes to the real thing, not the jeans, it is growing more difficult and costly to exercise true religion by the day.

Religion is being ghettoized. The First Amendment of our Constitution reads, "Congress shall make no laws respecting the establishment of religion, or prohibiting the free exercise thereof…"

That line has been misapplied so often that now the only place we seem free to exercise or speak of religion is in Christian caves and enclaves. Religion is for church, mosque, or synagogue, but it is taboo in almost any realm of public life.

Religion is an easy target. A movement of people who claim to love Jesus but hate the church has grown larger in the last few decades.

These are the ultra-cool and super-enlightened ones clothed in skinny jeans and adorned with WWJD bracelets. So tuned in to truth and so in need of a cause that they alone see the evil empire of "organized religion."

They even say the word "religion" like they are gagging on it. And they use snappy one-liners: "Jesus came to offer a relationship, not a religion!"

Religion can be abused. There is the very real problem of people who are religious hypocrites. People who go to church every week but whose lives are just as selfish and immoral as their neighbors who stay home.

And far worse than that, we are inundated almost daily with stories of murderers who use a demonic form of religion as an excuse to rape, torture, and destroy others.

And yet, for all of those glaring problems…

God is good with religion. James writes about *"religion that God our Father accepts…"*

The legitimate inference is that there is a religion that God accepts and even desires us to practice. We must avoid the temptation to spiritualize this fact away. The word that James uses for religion is a very specific word that means "external service, symbols, and ceremonies used to express devotion to a transcendent being."

James is talking about church, liturgy, and corporate worship.

Whenever faith is born in a human heart, the human heart will seek some way to externally express praise and devotion to God.

God called Abram, and what did he do? He immediately built an altar and worshipped Him.

God used Moses to lead Israel out of Egypt, and what's the first thing that God asked Israel to do when they arrived at the Promised Land? Build a temple with an altar and a prescribed way for them to relate to Him in worship.

When our Savior came to live among us, we read of Him: *"And Jesus, as was his habit, went to the synagogue."* Jesus went to church!

He lashed out at the hypocrisy of the Pharisees, saying, *"Woe to you Pharisees! For you tithe mint and rue and all manner of herbs, and pass by justice and the love of God. These you ought to have done, without leaving the others undone"* (Luke 11:42 NKJV). Christ never told them to stop practicing religion. He told them to be *authentically* religious.

Maybe you're thinking, "Yes, but that was before the cross and resurrection and the coming of the Holy Spirit. Everything changed after that." Well, during Jesus's last meal with His disciples, He said, *"This is my body given for you; do this in remembrance of me"* (Luke 22:19 NIV). He instituted a ceremony.

Then, when the Holy Spirit came and the church was born, Acts 2 tells us that they immediately began to meet in the temple court and break bread and eat together with glad and sincere hearts.

Hebrews 10:24-25 exhorts us, *"And let us consider how we may spur one another on toward love and good deeds, not giving up meeting together, as some are in the habit of doing, but encouraging one another—and all the more as you see the Day approaching"* (NIV).

If you think about it, any genuine love will seek to express itself through some symbol, form, ritual, or ceremony. When a man and a woman fall in love, they hold a ceremony to display their commitment to one another. Those rituals and ceremonies are not unimportant! Ladies, read this carefully: If you are in a relationship with a man who says something like, "Baby, we don't need a piece of paper, dresses and tuxedos, or a preacher to prove our love," then *run!*

True love demands outward expression, and that is what religion is meant to be. Songs, communion, prayer, Scripture reading—these are ways we outwardly express our love for God.

That being said…

God Is Not Good with All Religion

The phrase *"religion that God our Father accepts"* also implies that He doesn't accept all religion.

God rejects idolatry.

> *For although they knew God, they neither glorified him as God nor gave thanks to him, but their thinking became futile and their foolish hearts were darkened. Although they claimed to be wise, they became fools and exchanged the glory of the immortal God for images made to look like a mortal human being and birds and animals and reptiles.* ***(Romans 1:21-23 NIV)***

While pure religion has the power to uplift us, false religion has the power to degrade and cheapen us. Human beings are hardwired to worship, and if we won't worship the one true God, we will create an idol instead. If you reject the Lord, it doesn't mean you don't have a god; it just means you are going to worship a bunch of false gods.

The danger is that we always begin to take on the characteristics of what we worship. If we begin to worship creation, we will begin to act like creatures rather than human beings.

God rejects self-righteous religion.

Brothers and sisters, my heart's desire and prayer to God for the Israelites is that they may be saved. For I can testify about them that they are zealous for God, but their zeal is not based on knowledge. Since they did not know the righteousness of God and sought to establish their own, they did not submit to God's righteousness. **(Romans 10:1– 3 NIV)**

The Israelites were trying to establish their own righteousness. Any religion that approaches God by saying, "I'm a good person, therefore, you owe me heaven" is a religion that God does not accept.

God rejects dead, formal religion.

Having a form of godliness but denying its power. Have nothing to do with such people. **(2 Timothy 3:5 NIV)**

This is a religion that has a form. It shows up in church; it says the prayers, recites the creeds, and sings the songs. But it doesn't penetrate to the heart and shape the character of the person.

These people want their religion to behave. If you have a dog, you may have a kennel or crate to keep it in when you don't want it nosing around your business. Well, some people treat religion in the same way. They keep it locked in a crate and they only take it out for a Sunday morning stroll. They don't really believe that it should change their life. They deny God the right to use His power to transform them into the image of Christ.

So…

What Are the Components of Pure Religion?

James mentions two:

1. Inward component: Don't be polluted by the world.

This is a personal component of genuine faith. If you really love God, you will strive to live a pure life, be holy, and keep yourself from adopting or adapting to the world's standards. It will influence you morally, ethically, sexually, financially, and more.

2. Outward component: Look after widows and orphans in their distress.

If you really have a connection with the living God, it will show in your desire to express His love and kindness to the people around you. You will reach out to the hurting, the struggling, and the disenfranchised. Faith moves you to want to make some sort of difference in this world. Pure religion is going to do something in your heart that will not allow you to observe human suffering and remain idle about it.

Christianity is not a "hold on until you make it to heaven" plan. When Christ enters your life, He floods you with His compassion for the world, and more specifically for the community in which He has placed you. This is the part of the harvest that God has entrusted you with, and if He has touched your heart, you will feel a burden to make a difference wherever He has placed you.

As Matthew 22:37-39 recounts, *"Jesus replied: 'Love the Lord your God with all your heart and with all your soul and with all your mind.' This is the first and greatest commandment. And the second is like it: 'Love your neighbor as yourself'"* (NIV).

This verse sums up the two components that pure religion requires. And, unfortunately, many Christians—and entire churches—will embrace one to the neglect of the other. But it's not an either/or situation, as the scholar and author C. S. Lewis explained:

"You will find this again and again about Christianity: everyone is attracted by bits of it … that is why people who are fighting for quite opposite things can both say they are fighting for Christianity. Most of us do not really care what Christianity says: we are approaching it in hope of finding support for the views of our own party. We are looking for an ally—we are offered a Master."

So let's look at both components of pure religion.

1. Inward component: Personal purity

James implores us to keep ourselves *"from being polluted by the world"* (James 1:27 NIV).

A few years ago, Tom Cruise starred in a remake of the movie *War of the Worlds*. The premise of the movie is that aliens invade earth and begin to destroy everything. As the movie progresses, the aliens start dying off and no one understands why because none of our weapons seem to have been effective against them. As it turns out, there was something in the earth's air and soil that infected the aliens and killed them.

As believers, we are also pilgrims and aliens in this world. So we're walking around in an environment full of pathogens and pollutants that can destroy us. God has given us Christ and the gospel to create in us a holy resistance to these pollutants.

2 Peter 1:4 says, *"...he has given us his very great and precious promises, so that through them you may participate in the divine nature, having escaped the corruption in the world caused by evil desires"* (NIV).

Scripture is full of truth that can bring God's will to pass in every area of your life, but you're never going to be able to comprehend it unless you are truly cleansed by the power of Jesus.

The word "pure" that James uses in James 1:27 is from the same family of words where we get other words like "catharsis" and "catheter."

- *Catharsis* is a term that counselors use to describe someone who has had a deep emotional or spiritual experience that cleanses their mind from something that hurt them in their past.

- A *catheter* is a tube used in various medical procedures to help a body drain pollutants, waste, and toxins from the system when the body is unable to do it on its own.

Pure religion begins with a radical soul-cleansing experience. When God, because of love and by grace, comes into lives that are polluted with sin, caked over with selfishness, and infected by our own stupidity and lust, and He cleanses us, He purifies us!

"...the blood of Jesus, his Son, purifies us from all sin. If we claim to be without sin, we deceive ourselves and the truth is not in us. If we confess our sins, he is faithful and just and will forgive us our sins and purify us from all unrighteousness...He is the atoning sacrifice for our sins, and not only for ours but also for the sins of the whole world" (1 John 1:7-2:2 NIV).

Have you experienced that? You may have started attending church because your family is messed up, or your marriage is polluted by selfishness, or your kids are infected with rebellion and making you miserable.

The condition of your life—your marriage, your parenting, your finances, your job, your hobbies, etc.—depends on the condition of your heart.

Proverbs 4:23 says, *"Above all else, guard your heart, for everything you do flows from it"*(NIV).

If your heart is polluted, it doesn't matter what good works you do, or what rituals you observe, or how many acts of service you do. They're all useless if your heart is impure before God.

And the only way we can have a clean heart before God is to ask Him to cleanse us: *"If we confess our sins, he is faithful and just and will forgive us our sins and purify us from all unrighteousness"* (1 John 1:9 NIV).

That's where pure religion begins. As the old hymn goes, "What can wash away my sin? Nothing but the blood of Jesus."

Let me ask you: Have you accepted Christ? Have you experienced His soul-cleansing forgiveness? Has your heart been changed by the grace of the living Lord? If not, confess your helplessness and your hopelessness, and ask Him to wash away your sins.

Once a soul has authentically experienced that cleansing, the result will be that we will work to keep ourselves pure. *"All who have this hope in Him purify themselves, just as He is pure"* (1 John 3:3 NIV).

So the diagnostic questions are: Do you want to be holy? Do you want to please God in your interactions with people? Are you hungry for righteousness? Do you long for sexual purity? Are you making every effort to display the character of Christ?

This isn't about being perfect. That's impossible. But just because we can't obtain perfection doesn't mean we should be lackadaisical in our obedience to Christ. We must exercise ourselves daily to be godly. We have to want to *"perfect holiness in the fear of the Lord."* The more we do this, the more we will conform to the image of Jesus Christ.

No matter how you did last week, if your sins are forgiven and your desire is to please the Lord, then you are leading a life of pure religion.

2. Outward component: Personal compassion

The second component of pure religion is sharing the love of Christ through compassionately serving our world. Do this by reaching out, by getting involved, and by displaying His mercy to people who could never repay you.

James's words make this clear because of whom he tells us to help. He specifically mentions helping *"widows and orphans."* These were the most needy and vulnerable segments of society in James's day

So, we need to begin with the question, "What segment of our world, of our city, is the most neglected and overlooked? Where do they need us the most?"

James tells us to find the neediest people and to minister to them in their distress. "Distress" means "pressed or squeezed—nearly crushed." So James is not instructing us to focus on people who are struggling with mild discomforts and inconveniences. He wants us to help the person who is overburdened because life is literally crushing them under the weight of what they're going through and they have no way of helping themselves.

Stop and ask yourself: "Where is the most neglected neighborhood in my city? What excuses have I created to let myself off the hook for not being Jesus there? Where do people need me the most, even if they won't appreciate it?"

Then notice: How do we do it?

Even as I write these words, I can anticipate your thoughts, because I have thought them:

"Lord, I find myself praying just to keep my own house in order. I don't think I have the resources to change the world." The problems seem overwhelming and the challenges seem too large.

But, we can get started in some simple ways. We can pay attention to which governments and companies are being just and which are not. We can ask God to help us treat others fairly. We can at least have the courage to stand up for people who are being treated unfairly in our little world—in our school, our office, our neighborhood, and even maybe in our home.

We who have so much more than we need and deserve could give some of what we have to others who have no food, home, or hope.

We could stand up for the kid at school. Speak up for the neglected you know about. Serve the disenfranchised where you are.

It's a good start.

But James says we *"look after"* them. In other versions, that reads we "visit" them. Not just drop in, but visit as Jesus did when He became flesh and *"dwelt among us."* In another place we are exhorted this way: *"Have this mind among yourselves, which is yours in Christ Jesus, who, though he was in the form of God, did not count equality with God a thing to be grasped, but emptied himself, by taking the form of a servant, being born in the likeness of men"* (Philippians 2:5-7 ESV).

This is deep, personal involvement. It is more than throwing money at them. Our government has done that for years, and all it creates is dependency, debt, pride, and anger. James says we have to look after these people. That does not mean dropping by, writing a check, and going on our merry way. We have to be like Jesus, who *"dwelt among us."* We must go to them and make deep, sacrificial investments in their suffering and their questions and their fears and their hurts.

I know this is a lot to think about. I myself find it difficult to pray for my own household sometimes. There are many times I think, "God, I don't want to change the world today."

But God won't let us off the hook. And He won't let us try to love His world at arm's length.

In the spring of last year, a friend made me aware of a group based in Washington D.C. called the International Justice Mission (IJM). IJM is a passionate, Christian rescue operation that works to free victims of human trafficking all over the world.

We invited them to lead a conference in our church with the thought that soon we would be freeing slaves in many remote places. What we heard was that if you want to work for justice in your county, the best place to start is in the local foster care system. So we connected with Heartland for Children.

Heartland had just begun an initiative called 1–1–1. The idea was that one family from every single *one* of the churches in our county would take in *one* child and this would empty out the foster care system in the area. We presented the plan, and six families in our church agreed to take in a foster child. Two of those families took in three. Along with that, we began a ministry called Fostering Support, in which we train people in how to help those who have made this commitment. We offer them free babysitting, tutoring, prayer, support groups, and the like. That is an example of making an investment in those who cannot help themselves, and it requires personal sacrifice.

Keith and Bonnie Barker had been making mission trips to the nation of Honduras for years. But in 2011, during a visit to a government-run orphanage in that nation, God laid a burden on Keith's heart to start a children's home there that would partner with local churches and believers to show the love of Christ to these abandoned and forgotten girls.

So in 2011, Compelled By Christ Children's Home (CBC) was formed with the support of our church family as well as many friends and believers across the country.

Like most people who dare to walk with the Lord in His journey toward justice, the Barkers learned that Christ tends to reveal the path one step at a time. By 2013 CBC was home to fourteen girls—all of whom were rescued from some form of sex trafficking. None of them were older than seventeen. A few of them had shown up pregnant as a result of the rapes they had suffered. So, not only is CBC ministering to the girls, providing them schooling and job training, and connecting them to a local sister church nearby, but it is also the place where little babies have been born and saturated in prayers that God will break the generational curses and wickedness their mothers have suffered. The leaders of CBC work to see the Holy Spirit regain ground in these little girls' broken hearts, one painful inch at a time.

The Gift of Antonia

I often travel to Honduras with the leadership of CBC. We still visit the government-run homes to try to show these children whom the world has forgotten that God has not forgotten them. We roll up the remote dirt road and enter past a guarded gate into a compound that feels like a prison, where sin and selfishness have tried to lock away the memories of its responsibility.

As soon as our vans enter, children pour into the yard. They surround us. They hug our legs. They extend their arms, hoping we will pick them up and hold them. It is a joy to just be visited.

Occasionally we have room for one more girl in our home. That was the case on my last visit with CBC.

So, as we climb out of the van, smile, play, and hold little children, the whole team is praying for God to show us which one He sent us there to take back to CBC that day.

After a few minutes, the director escorted Keith and Bonnie back to her stuffy and crowded office. I was invited to come along. I slid past the trio talking at her desk and found a seat against a side wall.

The orphanage director was seated and motioned to her assistant to open the office door as Keith and Bonnie stepped to one side. Over the next thirty minutes, we were introduced to some of the girls. We heard some of their stories and prayed as we listened.

After the third girl left, there was a pause. Finally, Bonnie asked if there were any more for us to meet. The director hesitated, then gave a directive in Spanish to her assistant, who stepped outside. And we waited.

When the door opened again, all I saw from behind the director's desk was just the top of a head covered in thick, dark hair entering the room. Then, from behind the desk, a soft, timid voice whispered to the room, "*Hola, Dios los bendiga.*"

I couldn't help myself. I stood and peered over the director's shoulders at the voice that had captured the Barkers' attention. Looking back at me was a teenage Honduran girl who had walked into the room on her hands. Her legs were nothing more than stumps folded up underneath her body. Her name was Antonia.

And she smiled at me.

She kept smiling as she told us her story about being born with deformed legs. She was deemed unable to contribute to her family's income in any other way, so they made her a cut-rate prostitute and men from her village had paid the family to rape this little handicapped girl many, many times. Until she turned up pregnant.

Then the family dropped her off at this desolate home and left her there—and God brought her into that office to smile at me, tell me that horrible story, and tell me that she believed the Lord was still looking out for her.

Dear Lord, none of us had ever wanted to rescue a little girl so badly in our lives. But the director made us leave without that little girl that day because we didn't have a wheelchair for Antonia.

However, three months later, the Barkers returned with another team from our church and a wheelchair that one family had raised the money to purchase, and they wheeled Antonia out of that dingy orphanage. As Bonnie was pushing her chair toward the CBC vans, Antonia asked her to pause, gathered several of the other adolescent girls around her, and spent several minutes telling them that God would also send their rescuers.

Antonia gave birth to a baby boy at our CBC home last year. On my last visit, I was ushered upstairs to the room where she was cared for as she cared for him.

She placed him in my arms, and as I held him, she told me, "I named him Keith."

"Is not this the kind of fasting I have chosen: to loose the chains of injustice and untie the cords of the yoke, to set the oppressed free and break every yoke? Is it not to share your food with the hungry and to provide the poor wanderer with shelter—when you see the naked, to clothe them, and not to turn away from your own flesh and blood? Then your light will break forth like the dawn, and your healing will quickly appear; then your righteousness will go before you, and the glory of the Lord will be your rear guard. Then you will call, and the Lord will answer; you will cry for help, and he will say: 'Here am I'" (Isaiah 58:6-9 NIV).

If God can use true religion to make miracles happen in Honduras, He can make miracles happen in your own city. If you are compassionately engaged in living a life of holiness and committed to helping those who are burdened, the Lord will do amazing miracles in your midst.

Do you believe that? I hope so.

Today, God just might use you to be someone else's miracle.

CHAPTER THREE

Heaven and Hell

Then Jesus went through the towns and villages, teaching as he made his way to Jerusalem. Someone asked him, "Lord, are only a few people going to be saved?"

He said to them, "Make every effort to enter through the narrow door, because many, I tell you, will try to enter and will not be able to.

"Once the owner of the house gets up and closes the door, you will stand outside knocking and pleading, 'Sir, open the door for us.'

"But he will answer, 'I don't know you or where you come from.'

"Then you will say, 'We ate and drank with you, and you taught in our streets.'

*"But he will reply, 'I don't know you or where you come from. Away from me, all you evildoers!'" **(Luke 13:22-27 NIV)***

A young lady and young man fell in love, and the two were married. Soon, problems began to arise between them. Several of their disagreements were over issues of faith. The young lady had been raised to believe in Scripture. The young man hadn't.

Distraught, the girl called her godly mother.

"He doesn't believe in anything, Mom!" she wept over the phone. "He says he doesn't even believe in heaven or hell!"

"We can fix that," mom responded. "You convince him heaven is real, and I'll convince him there's a hell!"

Death and what happens after death are not comfortable topics. Most of us would just as soon not talk about these things.

Max Lucado called death "the big bully on the block of life. No matter how hard you try to avoid death or ignore him, sooner or later you're going to have to deal with him."

Forrest Gump said, "People had always told me that dying was a part of living. I wish that it wasn't." I think we'd all agree with him. Still, *"Sin entered the world and death through sin"* (Romans 5:12 NKJV).

Death was not a part of God's original plan for us. It wasn't a part of His design for humanity. So, if you feel weird about death, you should. You weren't designed to die. Which is why it's odd and uncomfortable to discuss. But here it is, and we do have to talk about it.

However, it probably isn't a discussion you want to be bushwhacked with in the midst of a crowd. That is what happens to Jesus.

Jesus is conducting His ministry in the midst of a lot of people while He is on his way to Jerusalem when some person, apparently without any social sensitivity at all, just blurts out a question on death and life after death!

Now, it's bad enough that this man brings up the topic in mixed company. But what makes it worse is Jesus's response to his question: Jesus acts like He knows the answer! Yes, there is a heaven and hell. And, He is even more specific! He has the gall to claim that He knows who will be saved and go to heaven and who won't be saved but will spend eternity in hell. None of that is acceptable in our eyes. This is the epitome of an untouchable topic.

We usually try to avoid this topic altogether. If we are forced to deal with it, we try to keep it as superficial and politically correct as possible.

One duty I perform often as a pastor is to conduct funerals. I've always been interested in hearing how people talk at them. Our speech is saturated with vague niceties: "Well, she's in a better place now." "He's not hurting any more." "She's happier now."

We say things like this because we don't know what else to say. But Christ is very direct and frank because the reality of death and the afterlife are far too crucial for us to approach for them with well-wishes and happy thoughts.

We need to know the truth even if it is unsettling—even if we don't like it. How else are we going to be prepared? So when this man asks Jesus about life and death and destiny, Jesus doesn't ignore the question. He gives a clear answer.

A Very "Human" Question

This question was nothing new. Jesus fielded questions about death, eternity, and our destinies all the time. He fielded them from all kinds of people from every walk of life. In just a few chapters, Luke will write to us about a man who approaches Jesus with this question: *"Good teacher, what must I do to inherit eternal life?"* (Luke 18:18). The man who asked that question was a rich, influential, well-placed man in society. But the question was the same.

No matter whether we are rich or poor, young or old, red or yellow or black or white, everyone eventually asks questions like:

- What happens to me after I die?

- If there is a heaven, who gets in and who gets left out?

- What happens to us if we get left out?

- If there is a heaven, what will it be like?

- If there is a hell, what will it be like?

We are made in the image and likeness of God, and we inherently understand that there is something beyond this world. So, like it or not, we're eager for news about another world.

Not only do we want to know because of something that we feel is true; we also *need* to know because of a fact we know is true: our time on earth is limited.

Jesus speaks of a time when *"the owner of the house gets up and closes the door"* (Luke 13:25). That is a way of saying that one day, your life will end.

We talk about "kicking the bucket," "assuming room temperature," or "taking a dirt nap." Jesus said, *"The door will be closed."* The point is, this life, and the opportunity it affords us, will not last forever. Someday the door will close!

This point is not comfortable, but it is not controversial. The evidence that we all are going to die is pretty conclusive. One preacher told me, "The death rate is still hovering right around 100 percent."

The Scriptures say, *"It is appointed unto men once to die…"* (Hebrews 9:27 KJV).

Woody Allen said, "I don't want to achieve immortality through my work; I want to achieve immortality by not dying." I like his idea, but it's not an option. We all must face death.

So here we are.

Created for eternity—and yet there is this undeniable fact of death. What happened? What is the explanation? More importantly, what do we do in response to all of this?

Destinations Are Determined in Advance

*Lord, are only a few people going to be saved? **(Luke 13:23 NIV)***

The problem with the question is in the way he asked it. This man wanted to have a philosophical discussion about eternity with Jesus. He asked in the same way we hear people ask, "I wonder how God will deal with people in deepest, darkest Africa who have never heard the gospel?" Or they ask whether you believe the "fire" mentioned in the New Testament is referring to literal flames or is just figurative language.

We like to have our discussions from a safe, sterile, intellectual distance. But Jesus hears the question and gets all worked up about it: *"Make every effort to enter through the narrow door, because many, I tell you, will try to enter and will not be able to"* (Luke 13:24 NIV).

You can almost see Jesus getting a little red-faced. "Do everything you can," He is saying. "Use every day you have! Get sweat on your soul over this. Pay attention!"

I'm sure that this person was probably taken aback by the intensity of Jesus's response. But Jesus knew something that we don't take seriously: our eternal destiny is hanging in the balance in this life. It is being determined by the choices that we make and the actions that we take this very moment.

> *For the Son of Man is going to come in his Father's glory with his angels, and then he will reward each person according to what they have done. **(Matthew 16:27 NIV)***

> *For we must all appear before the judgment seat of Christ, so that each of us may receive what is due us for the things done while in the body, whether good or bad. **(2 Corinthians 5:10 NIV)***

Two Eternal Options

There will be weeping there, and gnashing of teeth, when you see Abraham, Isaac and Jacob and all the prophets in the kingdom of God, but you yourselves thrown out. **(Luke 13:28 NIV)**

There are only two options in eternity. Just two. Jesus said to enter by the narrow way or get shut out. There's no middle ground. You either make it through the door into the master's house or you're left outside banging on the door, begging to be let in.

There's not going to be any nirvana. There's not going to be any reincarnation. There's not going to be any purgatory. You're going to heaven, or you're going to hell.

One of the greatest objections I have heard leveled against this teaching runs something like this: This doesn't seem to be fair. I mean, look, the average human lives seventy or eighty years. Maybe in that time we mess up, sin a little, make some mistakes. But, shouldn't the punishment fit the crime? Where is the justice in eternal punishment for temporal failures?

That seems logical to us because we simply do not understand our nature and the purpose of this life. Our destiny isn't about God keeping a score sheet throughout our days and then, at the end, tallying up the totals to decide who gets in and who doesn't.

Human beings are eternal, spiritual creatures. Something powerful is happening to us and in us as we walk and live in this temporal world. With every choice and action we are shaping our character. We are becoming more and more in harmony with God, or we are becoming more and more selfish and wicked.

C. S. Lewis explained it this way: "Good and evil increase at compound interest. That is why every decision we make is of such infinite importance. The smallest good act today establishes a point in our lives from which we may win victories we never dreamed of. In the same way, an apparently trivial indulgence in lust or anger today gives a foothold from which the enemy can move us into deeper darkness...each of us, at each moment, is progressing to becoming a heavenly creature or a hellish one. We Christians know people live forever and so we know that what matters are those marks and twists on the central, inside, part of our souls...we are becoming today what we will be forever."

That is why Jesus says, *"Make every effort."* That is why the Bible implores us, *"...purify ourselves from everything that contaminates...perfecting holiness out of reverence for God"* (2 Corinthians 7:1 NIV).

What we become today is what we will be forever. That's what this world is about.

The other day, my daughter had a sleepover and one of her friends brought modeling clay. And it got me thinking: You can make a lot of different things out of a lump of clay. You can make a coffee cup or a flowerpot or a figurine. It can mold into anything you want it to be.

But there will come a point when it hardens, and then you can't do anything else with it. The same is true of every person on this earth.

Facts About Hell

Like this man, we all tend to ask questions about eternity that are too simplistic. We do not have enough dimensions in our thinking to do better, I guess. For instance, when people say things like, "If God were really loving, then he couldn't send people to hell," that is a simplistic objection based upon a lack of understanding.

When this man asks Jesus, *"Are there only a few who will be saved?"* he is looking for a simple "yes or no" answer. He asks like it is a destiny with which we have nothing to do. So Jesus takes the time to explain.

We assume hell involves a unilateral decision—that God arbitrarily chooses who's going to be saved and who's going to be damned.

But Jesus's response to the man makes it clear that we have a part to play. It's our responsibility to do something. That's why Jesus says *"Make every effort."* Get ready.

In Matthew 25, Jesus says that someday people will stand in front of God and He'll say to them, *"Depart from me, you who are cursed, into the eternal fire prepared for the devil and his angels"* (Matthew 25:41).

2 Peter 3:9 says, *"The Lord is ... not willing that any should perish but that all should come to repentance"* (NKJV).

Those verses make these two things clear: God did not design hell for humans, and God does not desire that one single human go there. So, if hell was not God's plan for us and it is not His desire for us, why does anyone go there?

People choose to go to hell!

I will let you think about that for a moment because I know that you will read that line and think I wrote it while I was sniffing glue. But I really mean it. I need you to hang with me as I explain why it is true.

Look at how the people behave in the story Jesus tells. They are surprised. They protest. They believe the master of the house made a mistake in shutting them out.

No one ever thinks they deserve hell. Especially the people who go there! These folks don't see the door close and say, "Well, that makes sense. I mean, we had every opportunity. The door was standing there wide open for a long time and we ignored it. It is perfectly fair and logical."

No! They bang on the door and protest, "Lord, you made a mistake, we were good friends—come on, Lord, let us in!" No one thinks they deserve hell.

In fact, many in our country think that not only do they not deserve hell; they think no one deserves hell.

I sat at home one evening and made the mistake of turning on the news. Par for the course, I heard a horrible story about a man in Oklahoma who had raped an eleven-month-old baby and then murdered the child.

He was executed.

Most of us would utter in horror, "He deserved it."

No matter how liberal and open-minded you think you are, most of us would not have a problem with that man going to hell—if a hell exists.

Okay, the minute you admit that there may be one person who deserves hell, then you have admitted there may be more people who deserve hell. The only argument that remains is exactly what makes them deserving.

It reminds me of a quote I read from a man in Croatia who had seen his entire family raped and murdered by terrorists: "...it takes the quiet of a suburban, middle class home for the idea to be born of a God who refuses to judge."

But even if we can believe that some people deserve hell, *none of us thinks we deserve it*.

Those who chose hell protest, *"But we ate and drank in your presence and you taught in our streets."* They think that familiarity should get them into heaven. Ironically, that is exactly why they are left out.

Because they had all these opportunities sitting in the presence of God, yet they never truly embraced Him as Lord and Savior. They just went through the motions. And while days and opportunities passed, the compound interest of moral choices began to take their toll. Their character was being formed.

Does a Fish Know It Is Wet?

A few years ago, my brother and I took our families on vacation into the mountains of western North Carolina. The vacation home we had rented sat right on a small lake, and we had access to a boat. So every morning was committed to fishing.

I am not really a fisherman; my brother is. I went along and filled the time with daydreams. For instance, what did a fish think when my brother reeled it into our boat? I wondered if the fish would ever believe that we had good intentions for it. What if I could speak fish and make it an offer:

"Fish, we could give you a much better life than you have here living in this lake. We have a nice house. It's heated. We have nice couches and a big-screen TV." What more could a fish ask for?

I decided that no matter how much good I could offer that fish, it still viewed me as a threat and still had only one thought: "As soon as this guy takes his hook out of my mouth, I am going to get back in the water as quickly as I can."

You cannot make a fish desire anything better.

The same is true of people who have spent their lives resisting the grace of God. God can offer them heaven all day, but their character will be formed to the point that they will never desire it.

I tripped over the most incredible description of rebels in the book of Revelations:

> They were seared by the intense heat and they cursed the name of God, who had control over these plagues, but they refused to repent and glorify him.

> The fifth angel poured out his bowl on the throne of the beast, and its kingdom was plunged into darkness. People gnawed their tongues in agony and cursed the God of heaven because of their pains and their sores, but they refused to repent of what they had done. **(Revelation 16:9-11 NIV)**

People reach a point where they cannot and will not repent. Successful rebels. Even in torment, cursing the name of God. Characters set beyond the hope of redemption.

The Promise of Heaven

Charles Spurgeon used to tell young preachers, "When you preach about heaven, you must transform your face and show the full glory of God. When you preach about hell, your normal face will do."

We should be careful, because how we talk about the promise of heaven is so important. It is such a thrilling topic. Such an inspiring promise.

Bertrand Russell, a renowned skeptic of the early twentieth century, said that the idea of an endless life horrified him because it would be so boring. I am very sympathetic to his fears when I review the traditional ways we have been taught to think of the promise of heaven being full of fat angels and fluffy clouds and constant singing. That doesn't sound like fun.

But it also doesn't sound like the heaven we are promised:

"There is no need to be worried by facetious people who try to make the Christian hope of 'Heaven' ridiculous by saying they do not want 'to spend eternity playing harps.' The answer to such people is that if they cannot understand books written for grown-ups, they should not talk about them," C. S. Lewis observed.

I love the way Jesus talks about heaven. His descriptions are not spooky, weird, or ethereal. Here he says that we will take our *"places at the feast in the kingdom of God"* (Luke 13:29 NIV).

I can relate to that. Many of my best times and richest memories revolve around moments when our family came together for a huge feast.

It reminds me of Thanksgiving. We live 1,100 miles away from most of our family. So we pack up the car and endure a long journey toward home, full of anticipation. When we arrive, the day does not disappoint. We pull into the driveway and soon are standing at the door of the home, our hearts quickening to the muffled sound of laughter and conversation.

When we enter the room, every smell, every dish, every face unleashes a flood of memories. The nostalgia is so thick we can almost reach out and touch it. We share stories, and food, and laughter that is so long and hard our eyes are wet and our stomachs are sore. These are moments and feelings we wish would never come to an end.

Heaven is better than we can ever imagine. *God.* The God who knit you together in your mother's womb, who created your taste buds, who numbered your days, who knows everything about you. The God who understands the tears you cry when you're alone, who knows what makes you smile, who knows what brings you joy and captures your passion. The God who created the times you laughed until you cried and the sunsets that took your breath away. The God who flooded your heart with an indescribable wonder the first time you held your baby girl and she fell asleep with her head on your shoulder. That God.

Right now, He's in the kitchen getting ready for you to end your journey and show up to the big feast. A get-together filled with nostalgic conversations, precious people, and the smells and aromas of a lifetime of preserved prayers and memories. And new adventures.

And you will finally understand what Paul meant: *"'What no eye has seen, what no ear has heard, and what no human mind has conceived'—the things God has prepared for those who love him"* (1 Corinthians 2:9 NIV).

It will just be the beginning. It will be better than you can ever imagine. And it will never have to end.

The way to heaven is different than what we have been taught. Jesus ends His discussion of heaven in Luke chapter 13 by saying, *"Indeed there are those who are last who will be first, and first who will be last"* (Luke 13:30 NIV).

Of course, that is not the way things work in our economy, and it certainly isn't how they have worked at most of our family dinners. If you wanted the good stuff, if you wanted the best seats, you had to make sure that you hustled to get to the front of the line. To be first.

Jesus is teaching us, "The way you thought you were going to heaven is not the way you're actually getting in." We naturally assume that we have to work harder, do more good, and be better so that we crowd to the front of the line when the eternal rewards are being dished out.

But, no one is going to be seated at the marriage supper of the Lamb bragging about the size of their portion or their seat at the table. We're all going to be looking around saying, "How did I ever deserve to be here?" And then the Master of the feast will point to the Son at the end of the table with the wounds in His hands and say, "He made you worthy. He paid for and mailed your invitation."

The only people who get into heaven are the ones who fall on their knees and acknowledge Christ's grace. Heaven is not won, nor is it earned. Heaven is a gift given to those who respond to Christ and enter a relationship with Him.

Jesus says, *"I am the way and the truth and the life. No one comes to the Father except through me"* (John 14:6 NIV).

So I want to ask you right now: Do you know beyond a shadow of a doubt that your eternity is secure? If you die today, would you wake up in heaven? Or is that something you're still unsure about?

Heaven is not about works. It isn't about who finishes first or fastest or with the most religious ribbons pinned to their chest. It's about a free gift. All you do is ask, seek, and knock.

Have you ever asked for God's forgiveness? Have you ever invited Christ into your life? Have you ever fallen on your knees before Him and asked for the hope of eternal life? This life is temporary. You don't know when the doors will close.

We all need forgiveness of our sins so that we can know beyond a shadow of a doubt that we are saved, due to Christ's amazing sacrifice on the cross.

CHAPTER FOUR

Miracles

Is anyone among you in trouble? Let them pray. Is anyone happy? Let them sing songs of praise. Is anyone among you sick? Let them call the elders of the church to pray over them and anoint them with oil in the name of the Lord. And the prayer offered in faith will make the sick person well; the Lord will raise them up. If they have sinned, they will be forgiven. Therefore confess your sins to each other and pray for each other so that you may be healed. The prayer of a righteous person is powerful and effective. Elijah was a human being, even as we are. He prayed earnestly that it would not rain, and it did not rain on the land for three and a half years. Again he prayed, and the heavens gave rain, and the earth produced its crops. (James 5:13-18 NIV)

I was listening to a pastor, and he brought up an issue that had been a real tense one for me. I have spent a lot of time reading the Bible, and I'm astounded by the number of miracles recorded in its pages. Especially in the ministry of Jesus.

- He made blind people see.

- He made deaf people hear.

- He made mute people talk.

- He made lame people walk.

- He resurrected the dead (including Himself).

- He changed water into wine.

- He walked on water.

And that's just naming a few. John sums up his biography of Jesus by saying, *"Jesus did many other things as well. If every one of them were written down, I suppose that even the whole world would not have room for the books that would be written"* (John 21:25 NIV).

In other words, all of the jaw-dropping miracles that are recorded in the Bible are only a sampling! John gets even crazier. He relates that as Jesus was preparing to leave this earth, He told His followers, *"Whoever believes in me will do the works I have been doing, and they will do even greater things than these, because I am going to the Father"* (John 14:12 NIV).

So, if we believe Scripture, we should expect to see miracles. The truth is, we don't. Jesus crammed all these miracles into three years! Most of us would be happy if we experienced one miracle in three years.

So there is a huge difference in what we were promised and what we experience. That is an uncomfortable, untouchable truth that we would rather not discuss. Still, rather than ignore it, maybe we could be so bold as to begin praying, "God, help me to close the gap between what You promised I *should* experience and what I'm *actually* experiencing."

Once, Christ went on a mountain to pray with three of his disciples. When Jesus returned to the other nine, He found them desperately trying to cast a demon out of a young man. They couldn't do it. So Christ intervened and performed the miracle.

Afterward, the disciples asked, *"Why couldn't we drive it out?"* (Matthew 17:19 NIV).

I have asked that same question with different words often in my life. Maybe you have also.

"Lord, we prayed for her healing and she still died, why?"

"I have declared the power of addiction broken but I still got drunk."

"Father, we have fasted and prayed for provision and we are still getting foreclosed on."

Why don't we see more of the supernatural in our lives?

Jesus never performed two miracles the same way. Every miracle had some unique facet about it, which makes it challenging to write about this subject.

Sometimes you'll hear preachers say that if you just combine the right faith formula, miracles will happen. Like miracles are a religious hokey-pokey where, if you put the right thing in in the right order, that's what it's all about. But the truth is, there's no tried and true formula. Miracles are a mysterious thing.

So looking for secrets and keys is a futile exercise. However, I do think there is a lifestyle and an attitude that create an atmosphere that is more conducive to our seeing more of God's healing and powerful acts in our presence.

Start Expecting Miracles in Your Life

James begins His teaching with an obvious question: *"Is anyone among you in trouble? Let them pray. Is anyone happy? Let them sing songs of praise. Is anyone among you sick?"* (James 5:13-14 NIV).

We may not all look or act alike—we may be republican, democrat, Church of God, Baptist, Pentecostal, Black, White, Hispanic—but we all have one thing in common: We all have trouble in our lives. We all experience highs and lows. We all get sick. We all experience loss. So why is James asking such an obvious question?

Because we often do not think to pray about them. There is a disconnect between our real struggles and our faith. We walk through the week facing all these real and various struggles but never think to ask God to be a part of them. Then Sunday rolls around. We go to church, sing songs about the almighty God who can do anything, read a bible full of accounts of a living and loving God who comes into His children's lives and lavishes miracles on them. Then we say "amen" and exit the sanctuary to return to our ordinary lives, full of happiness, sadness, sickness, and struggle, but we leave God at church.

One saint said that we take thick, black, religious crayons in our hands and draw boundaries around God's activity.

Little "concentration camps" for Jesus.

This is not intentional stubbornness, but it is deadening to our faith no matter how sincere our beliefs. What has caused this weakening of our experience?

Three Reasons We Struggle to See Miracles

1. Bad Theology

Thomas Jefferson felt like the miracle accounts of Scripture were fables, so he cut them all out and reassembled a bible without the supernatural. That angers us if we trust the authority of God's Word. We would never dare use scissors to cut miracles out of the Scriptures. However, we have used doctrine to cut miracles out of our lives.

There is a whole school of thought that teaches that miracles were only for the apostolic age and that they are no longer a part of the Christian experience. That teaching has created people who adjust their theology rather than raise their expectations.

2. Weird Experiences

Sometimes we are hesitant to speak too much about the miraculous and divine because we have experienced people who act like that is the very air they breathe!

These are the ones who see the face of Jesus in their coffee grounds and believe God opened a parking space for them at Walmart. You feel antsy when the subject of miracles or healing arises because you're afraid you'll have to put on a tinfoil hat in order to experience the level of spirituality that these Christian friends have experienced.

3. Disappointment

This one is the most common—and real.

You've had times in your life where you did ask God for various miracles and healings, and nothing happened.

So you question the legitimacy of even asking. Or you begin to think God is powerful, but you're not spiritual enough to get his attention.

Listen, even the great apostle Paul had experiences like that. He writes about them with gut-level honesty:

"...I was given a thorn in my flesh, a messenger of Satan, to torment me. Three times I pleaded with the Lord to take it away from me. But he said to me, 'My grace is sufficient for you, for my power is made perfect in weakness'" (2 Corinthians 12:7-9 NIV).

This comes from a man whose life was filled with miracles. Right before this honest passage, he says, *"And I know that this man—whether in the body or apart from the body I do not know, but God knows—was caught up to paradise and heard inexpressible things, things that no one is permitted to tell"* (2 Corinthians 12:3-4 NIV).

So, in one passage, Paul says he has had supernatural encounters with God, and in the next breath, he is pleading with God for deliverance, but to no avail.

Just because God doesn't answer "yes" to every request for miracles and healing doesn't mean He has stopped healing altogether. So hearing a no on some occasions should not cause us to stop asking for a yes in every occasion. That is what James tells us to do.

How to Cultivate an Atmosphere for Miracles

1. Ask God for help in every struggle.

Look at how James says it: "If you are in trouble, pray to God. If you are happy, sing praise to God, if you are sick, pray to God for healing."

No matter what you're going through, you must always acknowledge God. You must turn to Him. You must lean on Him. You must make your requests known to Him. That is the atmosphere of miracles. Earlier in this same letter, James tells us, *"You do not have because you do not ask God"* (James 4:2 NIV).

That's pretty simple. God ought to be our first thought, not our last resort. But what do we do instead of calling upon Him? When we're in trouble, we call a lawyer. When we're confused, we call a counselor. When we're happy, we throw a party.

Maybe your marriage is on the rocks, or your kids are in rebellion, or your job is in jeopardy. Or (fill in the blank). And you lie awake at night, restless and full of worry. And although you're turning to counselors and having long conversations with friends, nothing is working.

Have you turned to God? Have you asked Him for help? Have you asked Him for healing? In order to cultivate an atmosphere for miracles, you must ask God to help you in every struggle.

2. Get along with other believers.

James 5:15-16 says, *"And the prayer offered in faith will make the sick person well; the Lord will raise them up. If they have sinned, they will be forgiven. Therefore confess your sins to each other and pray for each other so that you may be healed. The prayer of a righteous person is powerful and effective" (NIV).*

When have you ever seen Christians consistently practice this principle in the church? Have you ever seen a body of believers who are mature enough and holy enough to be able to do this with one another?

Now, let's be clear. This verse doesn't say to confess your sins to the priest or the preacher. It says to confess them to one another. This verse doesn't say to text that person's faults to your friends; it doesn't say to confess one another's sins to one another. That's not confession; that's gossip, and we have had that in the church for years! We call it prayer requests.

Gossip is one of the most destructive sins that exist in the body of Christ. It is one of the biggest reasons why we don't see more powerful manifestations of God and the Holy Spirit in the church.

Notice that James speaks of healing both in verse 15, *"...the prayer offered in faith will make the sick person well..."* and again in verse 16, *"...confess your sins to each other and pray for each other so that you may be healed."*

He is not being redundant. He is dealing with different types and levels of healing. We need healing as individuals, but we also need healing on a corporate level; entire churches need healing, whole families and communities need healing!

I assumed my first pastorate as a very young man (perhaps too young). I was leading a small congregation that met in a one-room church building surrounded by cornfields in northern Indiana.

I did not know much and we certainly didn't have much to offer, but over a period of three years I saw some of the most miraculous things occur in that church. I saw people healed at our altars. I saw several people born again. It was not an unusual thing for us to have services that lasted for hours because people were so caught up in the presence of the Holy Spirit.

Then it all came to an end. It just faded away and no amount of study or effort could revive it.

What ruined it? When did it start to go away? Most of the time, that atmosphere begins to die when the believers in the church get stupid and selfish with one another!

Feelings were hurt, misunderstandings didn't get settled, anger and bitterness set in. People started hanging around in the parking lot after church sharing their disagreements with decisions and their "prayer requests." Sister So-So is angry with Deacon Smith. The pulpit committee is disenchanted with the pastor.

You show up at church and see that person who you think cheated you or lied about you, so you sit clear on the other side of the sanctuary. If the Holy Spirit did show up, you wouldn't notice because you'd be too busy eyeballing that dirty so-and-so!

We offend one another and we are too proud to admit it. We get offended and we are too bitter to deal with it. And that poisonous gas of bitterness and gossip just kills everything in the church!

James brings this issue of how we relate to one another up over and over again in his writing:

> *My dear brothers and sisters, take note of this: Everyone should be quick to listen, slow to speak and slow to become angry, because human anger does not produce the righteousness that God desires.* ***(James 1:19-20 NIV)***

> *With the tongue we praise our Lord and Father, and with it we curse human beings, who have been made in God's likeness. Out of the same mouth come praise and cursing. My brothers and sisters, this should not be.* ***(James 3:9-10 NIV)***

> *What causes fights and quarrels among you? Don't they come from your desires that battle within you?* ***(James 4:1 NIV)***

> *Brothers and sisters, do not slander one another. Anyone who speaks against a brother or sister or judges them speaks against the law and judges it.* ***(James 4:11 NIV)***

> *Don't grumble against one another, brothers and sisters, or you will be judged. The Judge is standing at the door!* ***(James 5:9 NIV)***

James is emphatically warning the New Testament church: *learn to get along or the flow of God's blessing will cease.*

He isn't the only one who addresses this issue of getting along with believers. In Matthew 5:23-24, Jesus says, *"Therefore, if you are offering your gift at the altar and there remember that your brother or sister has something against you, leave your gift there in front of the altar. First go and be reconciled to them; then come and offer your gift" (NIV).*

I remember my mother taking my twin brother and me to Kmart for some back-to-school shopping. These shopping trips are always joyful occasions for both the mother and the children. So, in order to get us to behave, mom promised she would reward us by buying us one new toy after we had gotten all our needed clothes and supplies.

After what seemed like a century of shopping, the time had come and mom led us to the nirvana of the toy department.

The joy of being offered a toy was soon replaced with anger as my brother and I could not agree on one toy for the both of us. He wanted stupid toys!

Eventually it got to where I said "no" even if he picked a toy I liked, because I was mad at him.

Finally, after I had refused to compromise on a football, my mom ended the trip and we left Kmart with nothing. On the way out of the parking lot she snapped at us, "You boys can't get along with one another, so you're going home with nothing." And that's exactly what happened.

I think God deals with the church in the same way. If we all can't get along with one another, if we can't learn how to love one another, we won't get anything. It matters to God how we treat our brothers and sisters in Christ. So, if you've sinned against someone, make peace with that person. And if someone comes to you with a confession, God wants you to lavish forgiveness and love on him or her.

The Bible commands us to be kind to one another, to be tenderhearted, and to forgive each other just like Christ has forgiven us. We must love one another too much to give up on the relationship—no matter how uncomfortable it may be. Why? Because God is pleased when we get along with our brothers and sisters in Christ.

Let me ask you: What is the one thing standing between you and the miracle that you need in your life? Are you too immature to seek forgiveness from someone you've wronged? Do you find yourself gossiping about others? Do you avoid helping people in need?

The truth is, we all struggle with sin. We all mess up. We all do stupid things. We all make bad decisions. That is why we must show constant forgiveness and grace in order to create an atmosphere for the Holy Spirit to work.

3. Bold prayers

James finishes his directive on prayers for healing by reminding us of the story of Elijah. Remember, wicked King Ahab was rebelling against God's truth and ruining the land, so Elijah asked God to withhold rain until Ahab repented. And God did what Elijah asked. He withheld rain in the land for three and a half years.

Then Elijah prayed for rain to come, and God granted his request again. Think about that. Elijah asked God to change the weather and God did it!

That is the kind of faith we must exercise in the Lord. The crazier the request, the more glory God gets.

However, there is a difference between praying crazy prayers and praying like a crazy person. Let me explain.

When James instructs people to pray for one another's healing, it's pretty orderly and controlled. He tells the elders of the church to anoint people with oil and pray for their healing. He never says anything like, "Wave your jacket, and everyone on this side of the sanctuary will fall over. And then walk around the sanctuary until everyone starts laughing like hyenas."

You're not going to find instructions like that in the New Testament. I'm not saying there will never be unusual reactions, but the point is, that's not the focus. That's not what it takes to prove that God is doing something in our lives.

This *craving* that believers have to manufacture a super-spiritual atmosphere to prove that the Holy Spirit is active among us is wearying. I'm not saying expressing emotions is wrong. Not at all! If you want to laugh or cry or raise your hands, that's a truly beautiful thing.

But we shouldn't force that on anyone. We shouldn't be in the business of trying to whip up some sort of emotional frenzy, so we can all have spiritual chill bumps and talk about how great it was afterward at our favorite coffee shop.

So it isn't that we have to pray like crazy people, but we should be people who pray some really crazy prayers!

God says, *"Call to me and I will answer you and tell you great and unsearchable things you do not know"* (Jeremiah 33:3 NIV). Using that verse as a guide, make this your daily prayer: "God, show me great and mighty things that I've never experienced before in my life."

Psalm 2:8 says, *"Ask me, and I will make the nations your inheritance, the ends of the earth your possession" (NIV)*. In other words, God is saying: "Ask Me to give you power and influence over a nation and I will do it for you."

When John Knox started the reformation in Scotland, he prayed, "Lord, give me Scotland or I will die." What if believers started praying with that much passion? Again, Elijah asked God to make it stop raining, and it did for three and a half years. God is a powerful God! And He answers our prayers in mind-blowing ways.

We should pray that God would take over our families, our cities, our schools, even our government. That would truly be a miracle!

Again, in the sermon that started me thinking this way, Mark Batterson said, "Bold prayers honor God and God honors bold prayers."

God is not offended by your biggest dreams, nor is He put off by your boldest requests. Rather, He is offended when you don't trust Him enough to ask for His help.

I must confess, "bold" is not how I'd describe my prayer life. When I think about my prayers, they are pretty small and domesticated. Frankly, they are meaningless at times. I'll pray things like, "Lord, be with me today." What does that even mean? Or I'll pray, "Lord, just touch this person today." Or "Lord, keep us all safe today."

Don't slam this book closed! I am not attacking the small prayers. Jesus told us to pray "Thy kingdom come," in the same prayer that He told us to ask for our daily bread. God is interested in the little details of our lives. But oftentimes, that's all we pray about.

I'm not suggesting that we stop praying for our daily needs—and neither is God. I'm urging us to start praying bold prayers as well. Because when we do, it puts God's earthshaking power on display.

"Truly I tell you, if you have faith as small as a mustard seed, you can say to this mountain, 'Move from here to there,' and it will move. Nothing will be impossible for you" (Matthew 17:20 NIV).

You don't need huge faith and you don't need to be some sort of super-saint. James reminds us that *"Elijah was a human being, even as we are"* (James 5:17 NIV). It wasn't about Elijah. It was about God. The only thing God asks of us is our complete trust in Him.

So let me ask you: What big things are on your heart today? What challenges are you facing? What visions do you have for your family, for your school, for your church, for your city? What kind of redemption do you want to see?

Ephesians 3:20-21 says, *"Now to him who is able to do immeasurably more than all we ask or imagine, according to his power that is at work within us, to him be glory in the church and in Christ Jesus throughout all generations, for ever and ever! Amen"* (NIV).

Whatever the issue, God has the power to miraculously intercede in your life and help you with your problems. And remember, God's power is not reserved for the Billy Grahams and Mother Teresas of the world. It's meant for everyone who believes. So be bold in your prayers, and God will answer.

CHAPTER FIVE

Repentance

Have mercy on me, O God,
according to your unfailing love;
according to your great compassion
blot out my transgressions.
Wash away all my iniquity
and cleanse me from my sin.

For I know my transgressions,
and my sin is always before me.
Against you, you only, have I sinned
and done what is evil in your sight;
so you are right in your verdict
and justified when you judge.
Surely I was sinful at birth,
sinful from the time my mother conceived me.
Yet you desired faithfulness even in the womb;
you taught me wisdom in that secret place.

Cleanse me with hyssop, and I will be clean;
wash me, and I will be whiter than snow.
Let me hear joy and gladness;
let the bones you have crushed rejoice.
Hide your face from my sins
and blot out all my iniquity.

Create in me a pure heart, O God,
and renew a steadfast spirit within me.
Do not cast me from your presence
or take your Holy Spirit from me.
Restore to me the joy of your salvation
and grant me a willing spirit, to sustain me.

Then I will teach transgressors your ways,
so that sinners will turn back to you.
Deliver me from the guilt of bloodshed, O God,
you who are God my Savior,
and my tongue will sing of your righteousness.
Open my lips, Lord,
and my mouth will declare your praise.
You do not delight in sacrifice, or I would bring it;
you do not take pleasure in burnt offerings.
My sacrifice, O God, is a broken spirit;
a broken and contrite heart
you, God, will not despise. **(Psalms 51:1-17 NIV)**

In the last few years, both of my sons have graduated from high school. I gave them both the same gift. I let them choose any road trip they wanted in the continental United States. My oldest chose to drive Route 66, and my second son chose the Pacific Coast Highway.

If you've been on any kind of road trip, you understand the importance of music. Each trip had one rule. We each made a playlist of our favorite music, and whoever was driving, everyone else had to listen to their music. I did that to teach my boys some character. Kids today have it so easy; they have iPods so they can listen to whatever they want. They get to drive around in these little customized travel experiences.

When I was their age, I had to drive from Oklahoma to Indiana in a pickup truck with my father. My father's truck had an eight-track player, and he owned one eight-track. It was Merle Haggard. My dad's favorite song was "Okie from Muskogee." Do you know how weird it is for a sophomore in high school to know all the words to that song? So, to help my sons share in the pain, I made them listen to CCR, Three Dog Night, the Steve Miller Band, Dire Straits, and the Talking Heads, and they made me listen to—garbage.

Music is critical when you travel.

The Word of God tells us people of faith to *"[admit] that they [are] foreigners and strangers on earth. People who say such things show that they are looking for a country of their own"* (Hebrews 11:13-14 NIV).

1 Peter 2:11 urges us to live as *"foreigners and exiles…" (NIV).*

A pilgrim is someone who is traveling. This world is not where we belong. Our home is in heaven.

Like that old hymn: "We're marching through Immanuel's ground to fairer worlds on high."

And since that's the case, we need some traveling music.

In the book of Colossians, Paul tells the believers to let the peace of Christ rule in their hearts and to let the Word of God dwell among them—and he adds, *"Sing psalms and hymns and spiritual songs to God with thankful hearts"* (Colossians 3:15-16 NLT).

Apparently God knows that music is critical, because He inspired the compilation of the book of Psalms. Eugene Peterson called Psalms a "dog-eared songbook" used to encourage, guide, and direct spiritual pilgrims as we travel along the way.

The Hebrews sang these songs as they traveled and gathered for festivals and worship. These psalms were a reminder of the foundational realities that their lives were built upon.

Not every song is happy, however. When you come to Psalm 51, you are listening to one that is not lighthearted at all. Leonard Ravenhill said that this song was written through tears and punctuated with sobs. It is about the place where every journey with God begins.

Again, Eugene Peterson points out, "A person has to be thoroughly disgusted with the way things are to find the motivation to set out on the Christian way."

When King David wrote Psalm 51, he was sick of who he had become. For a year, he had been living a lie and he was tired—tired of the hypocrisy, worn out by the facade, sick of the pain, and disgusted with what his life had degenerated to.

This psalm is difficult. But it is his turnaround point, and if we learn it by heart, it can be our turning point also…

The Need for Repentance

I get to engage in quite a bit of counseling with people in various situations and stages of their lives. Oftentimes a person who is locked up in some great struggle will say something like, "I just wish I could get my life turned around."

We all understand what that means. We all have had that gnawing sense that life is going in the wrong direction—that it is slipping past us, and we need to turn around.

That is what the word "repentance" means. It is from a term that describes the act of turning around and going in a new direction once you realize you are headed the wrong way.

So, any time you want to get your life turned around, repentance is the first step. Both John the Baptist and Jesus began their ministries with this message, *"Repent, for the kingdom of heaven has come near"* (Matthew 3:2, Matthew 4:17).

On the day of Pentecost, the question was asked, *"What must we do to be saved?"* and Peter answered, *"Repent and be baptized"* (Acts 2:38).

The walk of faith always begins by rejecting your sinful ways and submitting to God's holy way.

Kisses and Tears

I have given you a dictionary definition and some scripture to introduce repentance. But knowing the dictionary definition of a word doesn't mean that you understand it.

The word "kiss" means to press together two sets of orbicular muscles in a state of contraction. The word "tear" is a drop of saline solution secreted from a duct in the eye.

Those definitions are accurate and technically correct, but they don't capture the meaning of a kiss or a tear, do they? To really understand a kiss, you have to pucker up and kiss someone. Once you have cried, you understand that a tear carries a ton of truth straight from a human heart and down their cheeks. That truth can never be captured in a dictionary definition.

So it is with repentance.

To understand it, you have to experience it, or interact with someone who has, and that is what is happening in Psalm 51. You are not reading a definition. You are experiencing the act!

Repentance Is Being Broken

David penned this song during the time in his life that is recorded in 2 Samuel 11-12. This *"man after God's own heart,"* who had been elevated to the position of King of Israel and blessed in so many ways, had sinned in a stunning way. He had slept with another man's wife and had that man murdered to cover up his adultery. After he had murdered the husband, Scripture tells us, *"David had her brought to his house, and she became his wife and bore him a son. But the thing David had done displeased the Lord"* (2 Samuel 11:27 NIV).

People probably thought David was a gracious king to take this poor widow to be his bride, but David was playing a game to cover up selfish and evil actions.

Repentance occurs when God breaks through all our acting and confronts the reality in our lives—the things we do in secret, the stuff we hide from everyone else.

One of the greatest hurdles we face in our spiritual lives is our desire to keep up appearances. Everywhere we go, we dress nice, we are a nice-looking couple, we have two nice-looking kids, a nice car, a nice home.

But God knows we have gaping holes in our lives. He knows about the wife who hasn't slept with her husband in three months and part of the reason is she suspects he is sleeping with someone else.

He knows about those kids who are angry and run off with friends to get smashed. He knows what dad looks at on the computer and where he goes after work. He sees a house that is mortgaged to the hilt by an unsustainable lifestyle and so we give to nothing outside ourselves because we are sucked dry by materialism.

He sees all of your sins, and He calls your bluff.

Repentance begins with a painful awakening to and an honest dealing with the unavoidable sin in our lives. Sometimes God uses a human instrument like Nathan to confront us, and sometimes it is just the painful consequences of our own sinfulness:

"When I kept silent, my bones wasted away through my groaning all day long. For day and night your hand was heavy on me; my strength was sapped as in the heat of summer" (Psalm 32:3-4 NIV).

Whenever we choose to live in unrepentant sin, and then cover it up or ignore it, God will lay His hands on us. And God has got some heavy hands! He can put the squeeze on you!

You will try to sleep and His finger will poke you awake and stir the guilt in your mind. You will try to prosper, and His hands will get into your pockets and snatch your prosperity.

You will feel the weight of the behavior you need to give up, confessions you need to make, relationships you need to end, and apologies you need to make.

Repentance happens when the Holy Spirit produces agony in your soul. Is God a sadist? No! Rather, *"the goodness of God that leads you to repentance"* (Romans 2:4 NKJV).

When God sees us destroying our lives and damning our souls, He uses pain like a megaphone. The sad thing is, we have the capacity to turn Him off. That's why Scripture is full of warnings like Hebrews 4:7: *"Today, if you hear his voice, do not harden your hearts"* (NIV).

We can become bitter. We can become defensive. We can harden our hearts. But if we truly repent, it is the beginning of our salvation.

The Nature of Repentance

We need to discuss this because there is such a thing as artificial repentance. We say the right things and bring the right sacrifices, but our hearts are not really touched.

Listen to David's cry: *"You do not take pleasure in burnt offerings. My sacrifice, O God, is a broken spirit; a broken and contrite heart you, God, will not despise"* (Psalm 51:16-17 NIV).

David pens those words because he knows that there is an artificial imposter for true repentance. It is all outward. It is all religious. We say the right things, we bring the right sacrifices, but our hearts are not really touched!

People are fooled by this all the time. They come to church, get emotional, make a trip to an altar, and have a good cry. Then they leave thinking their heart has been changed. They are deceived.

That sort of repentance may be therapeutic, but it is not transforming.

Paul told the Corinthians, *"Godly sorrow brings repentance that leads to salvation and leaves no regret, but worldly sorrow brings death"* (2 Corinthians 7:10 NIV).

That is what makes counterfeit repentance such a danger. You can feel bad about your sin, and still not truly repent. There are many reasons you can feel bad that have nothing to do with repentance.

1. You can be sorry because you got caught.

2. You can be sorry because of the way your life has been messed up.

Esau felt bad about selling Jacob his birthright once he experienced the consequences. But the Scriptures tell us, *"Even though he sought the blessing with tears, he could not change what he had done"* (Hebrews 12:17 NIV).

Why did Esau cry? He didn't want to stop being a jerk. He just wanted his birthright back. You have met people like this. They're not sorry they were sleeping around, but they're sure sorry they got pregnant. They don't want to treat their spouse better, but they sure would hate the public humiliation and financial cost of a divorce.

Those are examples of worldly sorrow. It doesn't lead to true repentance because it doesn't deal with the heart. God isn't interested in changing your circumstances. He's interested in molding your character.

The Nature of Genuine Repentance

For I know my transgressions, and my sin is always before me. Against you, you only, have I sinned and done what is evil in your sight; so you are right in your verdict and justified when you judge. Surely I was sinful at birth, sinful from the time my mother conceived me. Yet you desired faithfulness even in the womb; you taught me wisdom in that secret place. **(Psalm 51:3-6 NIV)**

This heartfelt prayer evidences all the characteristics of genuine repentance that leads to life. Notice all the personal pronouns in David's confession? See how he owns up to his sin? He says, "I sinned, and You are justified to judge me." Take note how:

1. **He doesn't blame anyone:** He doesn't offer lame justifications like, "My parents made me this way," or "My friends pressured me." And he doesn't say, "Besides, the hypocrites at church are no better."

2. **He doesn't justify his sin:** He doesn't say, "Sure, what I did was bad, but look at what they're doing."

3. **He doesn't rationalize his sin:** He doesn't say, "Well, certainly in another time and place, my behavior might be offensive and I can understand why it bothers You, but this is a different culture and You don't know all the circumstances."

1 John 1:9-10 says, *"If we confess our sins, he is faithful and just and will forgive us our sins and purify us from all unrighteousness. If we claim we have not sinned, we make him out to be a liar and his word is not in us"* (NIV).

God demands honest confessions. We have to be honest with ourselves and honest with Him. We have to get to our own hearts.

A Desire to Change

Cleanse me with hyssop, and I will be clean; wash me, and I will be whiter than snow. Let me hear joy and gladness; let the bones you have crushed rejoice. Hide your face from my sins and blot out all my iniquity. Create in me a pure heart, O God, and renew a steadfast spirit within me. ***(Psalm 51:7-10 NIV)***

David makes five critical requests of God:

1. To hide his face from all his sins.

2. To blot out all his iniquity.

3. To cleanse him.

4. To give him a clean heart.

5. To give him a steadfast spirit.

He is crying out, "Don't just forgive me, Lord. Transform me!" True repentance doesn't just look for different outcomes; it desires to be a different person.

When John the Baptist came preaching by the river Jordan, his message was *"Repent, for the kingdom of heaven is at hand..."*

Well, the Holy Spirit used that message to get some people's attention. Especially the words about repentance, and so the people asked, *"What should we do?"* John answered, *"Bring forth fruit in keeping with repentance."*

Then he got more specific: *"'Anyone who has two shirts should share with the one who has none, and anyone who has food should do the same.' Even tax collectors came to be baptized. 'Teacher,' they asked, 'what should we do?' 'Don't collect any more than you are required to,' he told them. Then some soldiers asked him, 'And what should we do?' He replied, 'Don't extort money and don't accuse people falsely—be content with your pay'"* (Luke 3:11-14 NIV).

John's point is, be transformed on every level: at home, in your politics, at your job. If you steal, stop. If you are selfish and stingy, share. If you cheated someone, make it right. Turn around and go in the other direction. This is what needs to happen. This is what God wants to do in you.

The Freedom of Repentance

Gordon MacDonald once said, "The freest person in the world is one with an open heart, a broken spirit, and a fresh new direction to travel in."

In other words, repentance is the first step to freeing up a bound Spirit.

Repentance brings real forgiveness and cleansing (Psalms 51:10). When you have been unfaithful, when you have aborted the child, when you have betrayed a friend, you can't go back and change your actions, or often even the outcomes. So, how will you ever feel whole, right, and worthwhile again?

Isaiah 1:18-19 says, *"'Come now, let us settle the matter,' says the Lord. 'Though your sins are like scarlet, they shall be as white as snow; though they are red as crimson, they shall be like wool. If you are willing and obedient, you will eat the good things of the land'"* (NIV).

It's a great freedom to know that your sins are forgiven, never to be brought against you again.

Repentance restores your communion with God (Psalm 51:11-12). When was the last time you felt joy in your salvation? When was the last time you felt a deep, personal intimacy with the Holy Spirit?

Our walk with God can dissolve into a joyless, duty-driven routine. Most of the time, we blame it on the church. The sermons are too long, the songs are too new, the Bible is too difficult, and so on.

If you don't have joy in your life, you need to do business with God. Peter told believers, *"Though you have not seen him, you love him; and even though you do not see him now, you believe in him and are filled with an inexpressible and glorious joy"* (1 Peter 1:8 NIV).

That doesn't mean you will walk around in perpetual giddiness laughing like a hyena. But it does mean that crankiness, depression, boredom, self-pity, anger, and cynicism will be the rare exceptions in a Christ-follower's life.

So, if your life is not characterized by joy, you may need to ask God, "Did I grieve the Holy Spirit? Is there something I did that needs to be fixed so You can restore my full communion with You?"

And it isn't just your communion with God that needs to be restored. It's your whole perception of life. When David says, *"Let the bones you have crushed rejoice,"* it is not referring to God literally crushing David's bones. The word "crushed" speaks to an emotional and spiritual feeling.

When you're in a state of sadness, it's impossible for you to hear any joy or see any good around you. But if your emotions are healed, your perception of life immediately changes! You hear joy again. You see hope again!

Repentance renews you to serve (Psalm 51:13, 18-19). After David engages in real, personal repentance, he prays for the country. If we want renewal for our country, it begins with us.

Once, in the nineteenth century, the *London Times* newspaper asked a number of writers for essays on the topic "What's Wrong with the World?" G. K. Chesterton, a well-known Christian author, sent in the shortest reply:

> Dear Sirs,
> I am.
> Sincerely yours,
> G. K. Chesterton

On our knees before God, peering into our own hearts—that is still the place to begin.

CHAPTER SIX

Holiness

Therefore, with minds that are alert and fully sober, set your hope on the grace to be brought to you when Jesus Christ is revealed at his coming. As obedient children, do not conform to the evil desires you had when you lived in ignorance. But just as he who called you is holy, so be holy in all you do; for it is written: "Be holy, because I am holy."

Since you call on a Father who judges each person's work impartially, live out your time as foreigners here in reverent fear. For you know that it was not with perishable things such as silver or gold that you were redeemed from the empty way of life handed down to you from your ancestors, but with the precious blood of Christ, a lamb without blemish or defect.

He was chosen before the creation of the world, but was revealed in these last times for your sake. Through him you believe in God, who raised him from the dead and glorified him, and so your faith and hope are in God.

Now that you have purified yourselves by obeying the truth so that you have a sincere love for each other, love one another deeply, from the heart. For you have been born again, not of perishable seed, but of imperishable, through the living and enduring word of God. (1 Peter 1:13-23 NIV)

I recently had to confess to my church that I am a lexophile.

They took it very well and responded with great grace. It isn't like they didn't know. A lexophile is a lover of words. So, I'm not a pervert, okay? I'm weird, but I'm not a pervert.

The fact that I'm a lexophile became something I could no longer deny after I spent hours reading and rereading an article I found on the Internet entitled "20 Great Old Words That We Should Use Again." It was a discussion of archaic words that once were in common usage in the English language, but now are obsolete. Here are a few examples:

- *Groak*: "To silently watch someone eat in hopes that they will invite you to join them." Now I know why I struggle so much emotionally. I'm constantly being groaked by my dog.

- *Hugger-mugger*: "To act in a secretive and deceptive fashion." So you can say, "I don't trust that guy. He's been hugger-muggering lately."

- *Snoutfair*: "A really good-looking person." Try that one out on your wife. "Hey baby, you are a total snoutfair." Oh—and then *duck*!

Once, these words were perfectly normal. But now, they sound odd, awkward, even weird. Why? We don't use them anymore. In this chapter, I want to reintroduce you to another word like that—"holiness." This word, which was once a profoundly relevant, precious, and beautiful description of our faith, has become a forgotten relic in the attic of doctrine.

I see some things that have contributed to that unfortunate reality.

Three Enemies of Holiness

1. Legalism

Legalism is the attitude and teaching that makes holiness all about hemlines and hairdos. The longer your skirt is, the holier you are. This approach leads to an angry, judgmental, and pharisaical lifestyle. It's legalism disguised as holiness. It doesn't make you holy. It often turns you into a hypocrite.

2. License

License is the idea that abuses God's grace. It takes the fact that we cannot do anything to earn our salvation and turns it into an excuse to not do anything at all. They allow grace to become an excuse to not seriously put ungodly behaviors to death in their lives. They neglect God's command to be holy, or at the very least, it turns into a secondary concern.

3. Relevance

Every one of us who has a desire to communicate the gospel to our world has a deep and legitimate desire to do that in a way that lost people can understand.

However, that desire can degenerate into an obsession with being cool, cutting-edge, and culturally sensitive to the detriment of clearly communicating God's teachings of holiness. There will always be something about genuine holiness that will be viewed as odd by our world.

As soon as you begin asserting biblical convictions about sexual purity, modesty, profanity, alcohol, generosity, sacrificial service, and entertainment choices, people will start looking at you like you just escaped from a *Leave it to Beaver* episode.

Still, even though we see so many shy away from pursuing holiness, I believe every human being has an unrecognized and deep hunger to be holy. They just don't understand it and they don't know how to begin to experience it.

Holiness Is Possible

If we had just met and I asked you to tell me about yourself, I'm guessing I'd know how you would answer. You'd tell me your name, how old you are, and what you do for a living. Then, you might tell me where you were born and what your childhood was like.

If I wanted to know you better and asked you about your character qualities, you might tell me that you are outgoing, shy, funny, adventurous, or curious.

I doubt seriously that you would tell me, "I'm a little bit shy, I like to fish—oh, and I'm holy."

People just don't talk like that, whether they are Christians or not. You'd never sit down at a job interview and say, "Hi, I'm Ed. I do good work. I'm punctual, and I'm especially good at being holy." That is more than odd or awkward. It sounds absurd.

Holiness is not a characteristic we think to aspire to. And, even if we did, once we understand what holiness is, it seems a bit out of our reach and presumptuous for us to claim to be holy. Or even aspire to be.

But I'll tell you what is even *more* absurd. Peter quotes a verse that tells us to be holy in the same way that God is holy!

We are not talking Mother Teresa or your Grandma. "Be holy even as I am holy!" You couldn't raise the bar any higher if you tried.

I have a friend who is a fabulous golfer. A while ago, he tried to teach me how to play. And frankly, I think he lost his salvation in the process. I am an awful golfer. As I tried to mimic my friend's golf swing, it reminded me of what it feels like to try to imitate God's holiness. Trying to mimic God's holiness feels like watching a professional golfer nailing a perfect drive, then looking at you and saying, "Do it like that." It seems impossible.

It feels impossible!

But, according to God, we can do it. God does not ask us to do things that he doesn't also make possible for us to do.

Grace Is Where Holiness Begins

Peter makes this clear with these qualifiers: *"But just as he who called you is holy..."* (1 Peter 1:15 NIV).

The command to be holy is only given to those who have heard and responded to the gracious call of God and been born again! Paul wrote to another group of new Christians, *"God chose you as firstfruits to be saved through the sanctifying work of the Spirit and through belief in truth. He **called** you to this through our gospel, that you might share in the glory of our Lord Jesus Christ"* (2 Thessalonians 2:13-14 NIV).

When I was a kid, I lived near a huge state forest, and sometimes we'd take school field trips there. The rangers assigned to guide our groups would always instruct us, "If you get lost, don't try to find your way back. Just wait until you hear someone calling you."

That's the concept. All of us were hopelessly lost, directionless, and helpless in our sins. The harder we worked, the faster we walked, the more lost we became. Nothing could save us, until one day we heard a call!

We felt that tug, that pull in the heart, that knowledge that we needed help and hope that was not available from anyone or anything other than God. That was the call!

Later in the chapter, Peter uses a familiar and even more radical word-picture to describe what happens to us.

"For you have been born again..." (1 Peter 1:23 NIV).

This description of our life was first used by Jesus when Nicodemus came to visit him one evening:

"'Rabbi, we know that you are a teacher who has come from God. For no one could perform the signs you are doing if God were not with him.'

"Jesus replied, 'Very truly I tell you, no one can see the kingdom of God unless they are born again'" (John 3:2-3 NIV).

This totally surprised Nicodemus, and he understood how impossible the request was so he responds the way any thoughtful person would:

"'How can someone be born when they are old?' Nicodemus asked. 'Surely they cannot enter a second time into their mother's womb to be born!'" (John 3:4 NIV).

Jesus understood his concerns; He knew that was impossible—that was Jesus's point. So He clarified: *"'Very truly I tell you, no one can enter the kingdom of God unless they are born of water and the Spirit. Flesh gives birth to flesh, but the Spirit gives birth to spirit. You should not be surprised at my saying, "You must be born again." The wind blows wherever it pleases. You hear its sound, but you cannot tell where it comes from or where it is going. So it is with everyone born of the Spirit'"* (John 3:5-8 NIV).

I have heard adolescents who were angry with their parents protest, "I didn't ask to be born, you know!"

And they are absolutely correct. They didn't ask to have life; they did nothing to get themselves here. They are on this earth kicking and screaming because a mother and a father made a decision and took an action for them:

"He was chosen before the creation of the world, but was revealed in these last times for your sake. Through him you believe in God, who raised him from the dead and glorified him, and so your faith and hope are in God" (1 Peter 1:20-21 NIV).

Just like you didn't choose to physically be born, you also didn't choose to be born again. You were born again because God made a decision on your behalf before you even existed:

2 Timothy 1:9 says, *"He has saved us and called us to a holy life—not because of anything we have done but because of his own purpose and grace. This grace was given us in Christ Jesus before the beginning of time…"* (NIV).

Grace is where holiness begins. Moreover…

Grace Is What Makes Holiness Possible

For you know that it was not with perishable things such as silver or gold that you were redeemed from the empty way of life handed down to you from your ancestors, but with the precious blood of Christ, a lamb without blemish or defect. **(1 Peter 1:18-19 NIV)**

Peter tells us that we are not just forgiven, we are redeemed. That word means you were bought from slavery! Slavery to what? Slavery to sin, slavery to selfishness and stupidity. Peter says you were bought out of slavery to that old, empty way of life.

God chose us and called us right where we were, no matter how messed up and lost we were. But his grace doesn't leave us there! He not only forgives, He redeems! He breaks the power of sin in our lives.

You have seriously misunderstood God's grace if all you see is that his grace saves you from hell. His grace also saves you from *sin*!

According to 2 Timothy 1:9, *"He has saved us and called us to a holy life—not because of anything we have done but because of his own purpose and grace"* (NIV).

Grace.

It is all grace from beginning to end. If we have been born again, and indwelt by his Spirit, we can be cleansed! We can put to death the deeds of our flesh! We can break addictions, and release hatred, and put aside filth.

We can be holy!

So What Does It Mean to Be Holy?

Holiness is peculiar. "Peculiar" is another way of saying someone or something is different or distinct. The word "holy" and all the words that are associated with it contain the idea of being separated from everything that is common. When God calls us to be holy, he is calling us to be radically different.

So Peter tells us, *"...do not conform to the evil desires you had when you lived in ignorance"* (1 Peter 1:14 NIV).

He is exhorting us, "Be different from what is considered normal in this world. Be distinct, set your yourself apart, and don't let this world force you to conform."

In another place, Paul said this: *"Do not conform to the pattern of this world, but be transformed by the renewing of your mind"* (Romans 12:2 NIV).

Peter points out that many of us just live a life mindlessly imitating the way things are done. A lifestyle that was *"handed down to you from your ancestors..."* (1 Peter 1:18 NIV). We just do what people have always done. We settle in and settle for being another one of whatever rolls off the assembly line of the world.

A world where it is normal to walk away from marriages, to spend all our money on bigger and better things for ourselves, and to go into debt so we are not and cannot be generous. A world where it is normal to use one another sexually and make sure our kids have all the right stuff, but ignore their hearts and faith.

We live in that sort of world. A floating mass of thoughts, ideas, values, and aspirations that constitute a real power and exert a real influence on our lives. "Don't conform to that!" Peter pleads...

So we are called to be distinct.

But being distinct is not just about ending our imitation of the world. Holiness requires us to begin trying to imitate our Lord:

"As he who called you is holy, you also be holy in all your conduct..." (1 Peter 1:15 NKJV).

That seems crazy, but that deep, radical transformation is the goal of our salvation. *"For those God foreknew he also predestined to be conformed to the image of his Son..."* (Romans 8:29 NIV).

That's what this whole life is about: you and I taking on the character of our Father, being made to look and act just like Jesus.

Holiness must be pursued. Notice the responsibility that is placed on us. *"Be holy!"* In other words, do something—take action! Holiness takes two forms in Scripture:

1. Positional holiness

When we answer the call of salvation, God forgives our sins, and we are forevermore seen as holy in His eyes.

2. Practical holiness

*...so be holy in all that you do. **(1 Peter 1:15 NIV)***

Once we're saved, we are motivated to pursue a life that conforms to the standard of Christ in our daily lives.

When the Holy Spirit enters your heart, you will begin to desire holiness. You will want to be sexually pure. You will want to handle your money in a Godly way. You will want to choose wholesome entertainment. You will want to treat your children with kindness.

We have to be very intentional about pursuing this sort of practical holiness in our lives. We are told *"Perfecting holiness in the fear of God"* (2 Corinthians 7:1 NKJV).

What is involved in pursuing holiness?

Holiness requires a transformed mind: *"Therefore with minds that are alert…"* That means that we need to have minds prepared for action. Minds so saturated with God's truth and God's values that we are ready to respond appropriately to all that this life will throw at us.

In another place, Paul tells us, *"Stand therefore, having girded your waist with truth…"* (Ephesians 6:14 NKJV).

You are in a battle. Decisions and temptations will come at you fast and furious. Make sure your mind is prepared for action. Get yourself full of God's truth so that you will respond in a way that is holy.

Holiness requires a sober mind: *"…and fully sober"* (1 Peter 1:13 NIV). "Sober" means exactly what you think it means. It speaks of the need to be free from the clouding influence of alcohol or any other depressant because they drag us away from God.

But in the broader sense, what Peter is saying is: "Be smart. Don't let anything have influence over you that would cloud your judgment and drag you away from holiness."

That influence for you could be money, or it could be a friendship. It could be a desire to own more than you can afford or it could be a romantic relationship.

There are some people you cannot be around. There are some things you cannot drink. There are some movies you cannot watch. There is a certain way you cannot dress. There are places you cannot be and maintain your control.

Holiness requires a mind with an eternal perspective.

> Set your hope on the grace to be brought to you when Jesus Christ is revealed at his coming. *(1 Peter 1:13 NIV)*

The primary reason we struggle so much in living holy in this life is we think so little about our eternal life.

I have heard people criticize believers by saying they are so heavenly minded, they are no earthly good. But the real problem is that we are so earthly minded, we are no good to heaven or anything under heaven. Eternal perspective gives us hope. It produces a reverent fear in us (1 Peter 1:17).

We will not live holy if we do not learn to set our hope on eternal life.

Holiness requires passion.

> Now that you have purified yourselves by obeying the truth so that you have a sincere love for each other, love one another deeply, from the heart. *(1 Peter 1:22 NIV)*

You see this often in Scripture. Especially in the New Testament. Whenever holiness is mentioned, love is really close by. John Wesley said that all holiness in life was "love aflame," or "love set on fire."

I am writing these words two days after having performed the wedding ceremony for two close friends.

I am thinking of the promises they made to one another: "I promise to honor you, I promise to serve you, I promise to comfort and keep you, I promise to forsake all others and cleave only to you so long as we both shall live."

Those are holy promises.

They reveal a heart of complete dedication. A promise of separation from all others in order to be totally committed to one person. Only a passionate heart can really mean those promises and keep them.

Is it any wonder that, back when we used to take those promises seriously, we called it holy matrimony?

Is it any wonder that Paul writes that husbands are to *"love your wives, just as Christ loved the church and gave himself up for her to make her holy..."* (Ephesians 5:25-26 NIV)?

Holiness is passion. We will never give ourselves fully to holiness if we are not passionately in love with God: *"I remember the devotion of your youth, how as a bride you loved me and followed me through the wilderness...* (Jeremiah 2:2 NIV).

And we will never be holy until we learn to sincerely love one another: *"...have sincere love for each other, love one another deeply, from the heart"* (1 Peter 1:22 NIV).

Sincere love manifests in my life by things I refuse to do and things I refuse to leave undone.

If I really love others, I won't steal from them. I would never violate another person's marriage by sleeping with their husband or wife. If I really love, I would never take advantage of another sexually, even if they gave me permission to!

If I love others, I will work to help them. I will passionately pursue justice for them. I will see to the needs of the "least of these" in my community. And most of all, I will try to share the gospel with them so they can have eternal life!

Be *holy*. Seek it with all you have. Don't ever quit. People spend their lives working for things of far less value. I promise you, if you make holiness your quest, God will give Himself to you in a way that will wash all questions away in deep assurance and joy.

CHAPTER SEVEN

Sexual Purity

As for other matters, brothers and sisters, we instructed you how to live in order to please God, as in fact you are living. Now we ask you and urge you in the Lord Jesus to do this more and more. For you know what instructions we gave you by the authority of the Lord Jesus.

It is God's will that you should be sanctified: that you should avoid sexual immorality; that each of you should learn to control your own body in a way that is holy and honorable, not in passionate lust like the pagans, who do not know God; and that in this matter no one should wrong or take advantage of a brother or sister. The Lord will punish all those who commit such sins, as we told you and warned you before. For God did not call us to be impure, but to live a holy life. **(1 Thessalonians 4:1-7 NIV)**

Human beings have always been sexually immoral. Paul wrote these words in the first century to believers who lived among friends and neighbors who indulged in adultery, homosexuality, prostitution, and premarital sex—all the same lustful passion we see today.

But here's the difference.

When Paul wrote these words, there seemed to be some consensus that there was something wrong with that behavior, whereas today, sexual behavior of any kind is considered normal—even encouraged. And those who don't accept this "anything goes" mentality are not understood at all.

As I write these words, I have just returned from a long family vacation. One of the blessings of those vacations is I watch very little TV, and cut way back on any sort of social media.

So I was interested when I saw that Russell Wilson, quarterback of the Seattle Seahawks, was making a lot of headlines. Not for playing football or for leading his team to back-to-back Super Bowls. Wilson was in the news because had stood in front of a congregation at a mega-church in San Diego and told them that he was not having sex with his supermodel fiancée until they were married. He said that they had made that decision because it was the Jesus way to do things.

Now, I am not going to dissect his theology, and I really know very little else about how consistently Wilson lives out that morality. But the public reaction is what I have found fascinating.

A mixture of sarcastic cynicism and angry accusations has greeted Wilson's statements. He has been accused of being gay. People have railed against his out-of-touch moralizing. All because a man dares to say he wants to try behaving himself sexually in a way that is consistent with the faith he claims.

That's the world we live in. Our culture mocks the concept of radical purity. And yet, that is the life that all Christ-followers are called to.

Paul wrote words to the believers in Thessalonica that will help us to achieve that godly desire in our lives. It begins with…

How You Think About Sex

All radical change in your life begins with how you think. How you behave sexually is the direct result of how you think sexually. So, if you are going to resist the world's way of living, you have to approach your life with thoughts and convictions that are steeped in God's truth.

"Do not conform to the pattern of this world, but be transformed by the renewing of your mind" (Romans 12:2 NIV).

Paul makes his appeal for us to live in a way that *"pleases God."* In a way that is *"holy and honorable."* He does not base that appeal on guilt or emotion but on truth. Truth we do not hear often.

Your Sex Life Is Important to God

I can see your eyes rolling! (Well, I can imagine your eyes are rolling) I know it sounds crazy, and maybe it even makes you uncomfortable, but it's true. We only react the way we do because we have neglected speaking about this in our churches or thinking about it in the presence of God.

Paul writes, *"It is God's will that you should be sanctified: that you should avoid sexual immorality; that each of you should learn to control your own body in a way that is holy and honorable..."* (1 Thessalonians 4:3-4 NIV).

He brings up sex and uses the word "sanctification" to talk about it. "Sanctification" is the last word we think belongs in a conversation about sex! That word is so religious it smells like a church pew. What does it have to do with sex?

That is the problem.

We leave our core beliefs at church, or debate them in seminary class rooms, but never learn what we are supposed to do about them. How do we live them?

This verse begins, *"This is God's will..."* All of us have uttered, "I just wish I knew what the will of the Lord is. I just wish I could figure what God wants." Well, here is a place where we are told, "This is the Lord's will!" That we be sanctified. This is not a church word: it is a relationship word. It means "to be set apart for a purpose."

The best way I can understand it is to think about my favorite coffee mug. I love that mug. It is *my mug*. I chose it from all the other mugs to use for one thing: to drink coffee.

I marched my family into the kitchen and showed them the mug. I declared, "This mug is for coffee. Woe be unto the child that uses my special mug to pour into it and drink from it the juice of the orange or the milk of the bovine! In the day thou doest that, you shall surely die!"

They weren't impressed.

But they understood how passionate I am about that mug. They knew that I had set it apart for one use and didn't want it misused.

In the same way, God has chosen us and He has set us apart to live in a very specific way. God's will is that we would belong uniquely to Him and live to serve His purposes. That's what it means to be sanctified.

These words of our faith like "sanctification" and "holiness" are not Sunday school words. They are living room words. They are board room words. They are bedroom words. For they address how we think and work and live.

In the last week, you may not have thought much about the GDP of China and how it is affecting our economy. You probably haven't given a lot of thought to your theology of the Second Coming—whether you are pre-, post-, or amillenial.

But I can almost guarantee that you have thought about sex.

My point is that your faith in God and your relationship to God through Christ are meant to have an impact on your *life*! And sex is a pretty important part of your life. So God clearly expresses His will for that part of life very clearly.

God's Will for Your Sex Life

As for other matters, brothers and sisters, we instructed you how to live in order to please God...It is God's will that you should be sanctified: that you should avoid sexual immorality... For God did not call us to be impure, but to live a holy life. (1 Thessalonians 4:1, 3, 7 NIV)

Words like "immorality" sound odd nowadays. There is not much room in our modern thinking for that concept.

We live by the credos "What I do with my body is my business" and "Whatever is done between consenting adults is their business." So a common response to any appeal for sexual purity is rebuke: "Don't try to impose your morality on me!"

However, we cannot live by those standards. My body is not just my business because I am not my own, I have been bought with a price. I cannot sink to the philosophy of "whatever happens between two adults" because I have to think of more than their consent; I have to think of God's will.

Simply put, God says that some behavior pleases Him and some angers Him. Some sexual behavior is good and holy and other sexual behavior is impure and immoral. Some lifestyles uplift and build up, and other lifestyles degrade and tear down. If I want to please God, I will chose His will about sex over my own ideas or the ideas of this culture.

And there really are great reasons why.

A Beautiful Purpose

Why does God snoop around in our sex lives? Why does purity matter so much to Him? Well, God would not be interested in anything that wasn't important to Him and extremely important to us as humans.

Let me state the obvious. Sex was God's idea. I remember reading a great line that Brian Wilkerson wrote: "It isn't like Adam and Eve came running out of the bushes one day, all red-faced and breathless, and said to God, 'You will never believe what we came up with.'"

God came up with the idea, and He did so with a plan in mind.

"The Lord God said, 'It is not good for the man to be alone. I will make a helper suitable for him.' Now the Lord God had formed out of the ground all the wild animals and all the birds in the sky. He brought them to the man to see what he would name them; and whatever the man called each living creature, that was its name. So the man gave names to all the livestock, the birds in the sky and all the wild animals. But for Adam no suitable helper was found. So the Lord God caused the man to fall into a deep sleep; and while he was sleeping, he took one of the man's ribs and then closed up the place with flesh. Then the Lord God made a woman from the rib he had taken out of the man, and he brought her to the man" (Genesis 2:18-22 NIV).

If you are a parent, you have to love this story. Have you ever found the perfect Christmas gift for your kids?

On Christmas Eve, you tuck them in their beds. Then you wrap the gifts, place them under the tree, and go to bed yourself. *But you are the one who can't sleep!* You cannot wait to see their joyful reaction and hear their laughter when they see the gift you got for them the next morning.

I think that's how God felt about presenting Eve to Adam. He put Adam to sleep, then He created the perfect gift for him.

And when the morning came, He *"brought the woman to the man."* You gotta love that! All the other animals just "pass before" Adam so he can hang a name on them. But when it is time for the woman, God *"brought her to the man."* This is significant. God wanted to see Adam's face when he beheld Eve for the first time.

And here is Adam, naming animals. Maybe he has reached the D's—"Dog … donkey … duck-billed platypus…" Then God shows him the woman: "Wow!"

The writer explains, *"For this reason…"* In other words, this is why we act the way we do. This is why we fall in love and write songs and poems. This is why we get jealous, get engaged, get married. This is the reason God did it. God created woman especially for man."

Why?

The story begins, *"The Lord God said, 'It is not good for the man to be alone.'"* That is the first time you hear God say "not good." Our "aloneness" is not good. There are things that are necessary for us that only intimacy with another human being can provide. So one reason God created us and hardwired us to desire sex was because sex is His pathway to establishing the deepest level of intimacy between two human beings.

The purpose of sex is to serve as a magnet to pull a man and a woman together and make them inseparable, intimate, and trusting.

One writer says, "God created Eve by removing her from Adam's side and none of us had ever recovered from that surgery. We are all looking to be reunited with someone. To be deeply and truly known. To have someone in our lives with whom a simple glance is all that is needed to communicate what is in my heart."

That is why God created sex.

So it's understandable why God gets angry when people treat His wonderful gift as a recreational sport driven by hormones and selfishness.

The movie *A Beautiful Mind* is a story about a man who is a mentally imbalanced genius. In one scene, he and his buddies are at a bar. The man's friends dare him to try and pick up a woman. So he walks over and sits next to her at the bar.

After a few seconds of awkward silence, he says, "I don't exactly know what I need to say in order for us to have intercourse, but can we just assume that I have said those things? I mean, essentially, aren't we just talking about fluid exchange?" He got slapped. He deserved it. But, though we are not so direct or coarse, those words really do capture the way we approach sex. We have so cheapened it.

When Myron Augsberger was pastoring in the D.C. area, he was invited to take part in an after-hours business event. He took a seat at a table and was introduced to a gentleman who, when he learned what Augsberger did, said, "I really don't like preachers very much."

Augsberger replied, "That's good. I don't like most of them I meet either." And then Augsberger said, "Listen, why don't you think about coming to church with me sometime?"

The man said, "I'll think about it, but tell me one thing. What do you think about sex?"

"I'm in favor of it," Augsberger answered.

The man smiled and extended his hand "Hey, you're my kind of preacher."

"Wait a second, you need to understand," Augsberger said as he grasped his hand for a moment, "I'm in favor of it, but I think too much of it to cheapen it the way our culture does." So should we all. We should live out of deep respect and gratefulness for God and this gift—*"not in passionate lust like the pagans, who do not know God..."*

How to Remain Sexually Pure

1. Be passionate for God.

...live in order to please God... (1 Thessalonians 4:1 NIV)

Paul doesn't begin his appeal for sexual purity with warnings about how you might get some disease, or how you might end up pregnant, or how you might be embarrassed. He begins by encouraging you to fall deeper in love with your God and become passionate to please Him. That is the best way to ward off an immoral lifestyle.

Scripture says we must learn to control our own bodies in a way that is holy and honorable. Holiness is not an invitation for you to grit your teeth and resist temptation. Holiness is an invitation for you to fall head-over-heels in love with God.

2. Love others.

"No one should wrong or take advantage of a brother or sister."

If you're going to maintain yourself sexually, you need to love others like Jesus does. If I have sex with someone outside of a committed marriage, I am not loving them: I am using them. I am taking advantage of them for selfish gratification. That is true even if they are a consenting adult.

There was a line in a Bob Seger song: "I used her, and she used me, but neither one cared. We were gettin' our share."

But Paul says, "That is how a pagan thinks! Not someone who knows God!" And if you know God and understand his will, then for you to have sex with anyone you are not absolutely committed to for a lifetime is taking advantage of and cheating them. It is selfish and destructive.

Refusing to know God, Paul says in Romans 1:26, they soon didn't know how to be human either—women didn't know how to be women; men didn't know how to be men. Sexually confused, they *abused and defiled one another*, women with women and men with men—*all lust and no love*.

Remember Genesis 2:24? It says, *"That is why a man leaves his father and mother and is united to his wife, and they become one flesh" (NIV).* The Hebrew word there means "glued together." You have glued two pieces of paper together. When you let it dry, and then try pulling them apart, no matter how careful you are, the papers rip—and not cleanly. That will happen every single time, whether you like it or not.

When you sleep with someone, your body makes a promise, even if you're not making a promise. You become attached to them, and when absolute commitment is lacking, there will be tears in the soul. It cannot be avoided.

3. Be self-controlled.

...each of you should learn to control your own body in a way that is holy and honorable. (1 Thessalonians 4:4 NIV)

If we are going to honor God and respect others in this world, we have to be intentional. Paul says we need to learn how to be self-controlled.

So, being sexually pure will requires learning, thinking, planning. You have to know how you operate.

What are your weak areas? It's not about intellect; it's about discipline. Paul says, *"Flee from sexual immorality"* (1 Corinthians 6:18 NIV). That word "flee" means to run as fast as you can away from sexual immorality.

I attended a church meeting once where I had to do some church discipline. The room we met in was small, and the atmosphere was tense and a bit combative. I was outnumbered, and I hate to admit it, but while I was praying I was wondering, "What are they going to do to me when I tell them the hard truth?"

And so you know what I did? I prayed with one eye open looking for the nearest door. I was thinking, "If I have to run, I want to know how to get out of here."

So when Paul tells Christians to flee from sexual immorality, he is essentially saying, "You better understand the danger. You better be thinking ahead. You better know where you're going to run before you get in trouble."

Pastor Craig Groeschel offered some terrific, practical strategies to single believers that will help them control themselves in ways that are holy and honorable:

1. Dress for success.

In other words, don't put out an ad unless you want someone to answer. Don't try to entice people with the way you dress.

2. Keep all four on the floor.

When you're with your boyfriend or girlfriend, both of you keep your feet on the floor. How is that for practical advice?

3. You're too old for sleepovers.

Sleepovers end in the sixth grade. You might be tempted to think, "Oh, it's so far to drive and it's so late." I encourage you: Get in your car and go home.

4. No tonsil hockey.

Enough said.

5. Avoid dangerous places and situations.

You know where you shouldn't be and you know why you're going there before you go. Tell yourself the truth and avoid dangerous situations.

6. Guard your eyes.

What are you looking at? What do you pay attention to? If someone could read your mind, would you be ashamed?

Of course, it isn't just single people who need this. We all have to learn to live this way. That means we have to learn his will and truth and have a plan.

But that also means that there are many in the church who haven't learned to live that way. There were people in Thessalonica who were hearing these things for the first time. They had never believed that way or lived that way.

Many of them had lived immoral lives. They had things in their background they were terribly ashamed of and embarrassed about.

But the good news then and now is this: Because of God's grace, it is never too late to start over and start learning this new and wonderful way of living sexually.

CHAPTER EIGHT

Generosity

Do not store up for yourselves treasures on earth, where moths and vermin destroy, and where thieves break in and steal. But store up for yourselves treasures in heaven, where moths and vermin do not destroy, and where thieves do not break in and steal. For where your treasure is, there your heart will be also. **(Matthew 6:19-21 NIV)**

In my years preaching, I have learned there are two topics that people are especially touchy about: sex and money.

Funny thing is, the resistance to preaching about sex has declined. In fact, people seem to desire to learn more about what Scripture teaches concerning God's will for sex. But, the money thing is still a problem. So…

Now, we are going to talk about money.

There I said it: MONEY, MONEY, MONEY!

In the following pages, I'm going to teach you how to deal with your finances. And if you are apprehensive and wondering what that means, let me see if I can put you at ease first by telling you what it doesn't mean.

I will not be telling you how to get more money. I own (and when I say "own," I mean, "I am paying for") three cars, and the newest one is seven years old. I am trying to put two sons through college, and I have an adolescent daughter. Enough said. I don't have any "champagne wishes and caviar dreams" to sell you.

I also will not be telling you how to protect the money you have. We hear a great deal about that in these uncertain times. We obsess over protecting our assets and preserving our savings. We give away a lot of our money to people who will tell us how to keep our money.

I am not qualified or concerned with telling you how to protect your money; my goal is to talk with you about how to protect your heart from your money.

Money Is God's Chief Competition for Your Heart

> *No one can serve two masters. Either you will hate the one and love the other, or you will be devoted to the one and despise the other. You cannot serve both God and money.*
> **(Matthew 6:24 NIV)**

If I walked out of my office this minute and did a random man-on-the-street interview with ten believers, asking them to name the greatest enemy of their faith, I bet eight out of ten would answer, "The devil!" But I don't think that's the right answer.

I know beyond a shadow of a doubt that the devil is a real and dangerous enemy. The Bible says he roams about like a roaring lion, seeking whom he may devour. But, he's not our *only* enemy. I personally don't believe he's our worst enemy.

The reformers taught that Christians face three great enemies: the world, the flesh, and the devil. We tend to give the devil credit for stuff that he didn't have any part of. We're capable of messing up our lives all on our own without any assistance from the devil.

When it comes to money, we are dealing with *"service and devotion,"* according to Jesus. Those are words of worship.

I doubt that any person reading this book consciously has to wrestle with whether they are going to worship the devil. If you do, you need a different book. But all of us do wrestle with an inordinate trust in and pursuit of money.

If I were to ask you for a quarter, you wouldn't bat an eye, right? If I asked you for ten dollars, you might raise your eyebrows, but you'd probably give it to me. But what if I asked you for fifty dollars? Or one hundred?

At some point, letting go of money will cause us to cringe and grow uneasy, defensive, and angry.

That's because even though money is just material in itself, we attach things of huge importance to money. Things like power, security, and sense of importance and achievement. The problem isn't with the paper the money is printed on. The problem is with a spirit that attaches to money.

The Demon of Our Culture

In the King James Version, Matthew 6:24 reads, *"Ye cannot serve God and mammon."*

Mammon was the name of a demon or a spirit that people believed would literally attach itself to money. There is such a spirit. We call it greed.

Greed is the demon of our culture. It's the atmosphere in which we live that subtly corrupts our values.

Sometimes I ask my kids, "Does a fish know it's wet?" Of course not. If I asked you if you were greedy, you'd probably say, "Absolutely not!"

But you are.

We all are, because our culture produces greedy people—and we're not even aware of it. That's why Jesus warns us: *"So do not worry saying, 'What shall we eat?' or 'What shall we drink?' or 'What shall we wear?' For the pagans run after all these things..."* (Matthew 6:31-32 NIV).

Jesus's great concern is that we will become just like the pagans. Because we live in a culture of greed, we will begin to live like greedy people around us in the way we approach, earn, use, and value money.

I grew up attending a church that was a part of a very strict, conservative, "holiness" denomination. They were very concerned that we not become worldly. That is a valid concern. The problem was that they defined and detected "worldliness" in hemlines and hairdos and Hollywood. Our dangers were in movies and sensual clothing and the like.

Well, I agree that the overwhelming amount of stuff produced in Hollywood is worthless. I agree that we need to try to be modest and respectful in dress. However, worldliness has far more to do with our attitude toward, pursuit of, and use of money than it does those things.

You can dress like a puritan and still have the values of a pagan.

And that is…

Our Greatest Danger

"But store up for yourselves treasures in heaven…"
(Matthew 6:20 NIV)

One of the greatest dangers that Christians face is the failure to realize that we will be judged in this life—not only for the sins that we commit, but also for the things we knew we should've done and didn't. This is especially true in our use of money.

When Jesus tells us to use our money and resources to *"store up…treasures in heaven,"* He is indicating that somehow our eternity is impacted by our use or misuse of money.

Then He says, *"The eye is the lamp of the body. If your eyes are healthy, your whole body will be full of light. But if your eyes are unhealthy, your whole body will be full of darkness. If then the light within you is darkness, how great is that darkness!"* (Matthew 6:22-23 NIV).

Basically, what that means is, when your view of money gets messed up, your whole perspective on life gets messed up, too.

I had to take a basic psychology class when I was in in college. I have never forgotten our professor describing an experiment that was conducted at the University of California, Berkeley. They put pieces of corn in front of chickens to see how they would peck at the corn. Then they created little chicken glasses that warped the chicken's view so they would see the corn three inches to the right of where it actually was.

My first thought was, "That is exactly the kind of thing you would expect to be happening at California, Berkley." But I digress.

What they discovered was that the chickens almost never made the adjustment. They would just keep banging their beaks into the dirt at what they thought was the prize. Just pounded their heads into the ground and never attained anything that would satisfy their legitimate hunger.

And I wondered, "Are humans any smarter than those chickens?" So often our thoughts about what we need and how money can help us attain them are warped. We think we have a bead on the thing that will satisfy our desires. So, with our eyes on that illusory prize, we spend our days banging our heads against the wall and never satisfying our hunger.

How do we avoid that fate? What is the remedy?

Jesus says we need to lay up treasures for ourselves in heaven. How do we do that? And why is it so important?

"Command those who are rich in this present world not to be arrogant nor to put their hope in wealth, which is so uncertain, but to put their hope in God, who richly provides us with everything for our enjoyment. Command them to do good, to be rich in good deeds, and to be generous and willing to share. In this way they will lay up treasure for themselves as a firm foundation for the coming age, so that they may take hold of the life that is truly life" (1 Timothy 6:17-19 NIV).

When we see and use money as a way to serve God and bless others, that is how we lay up treasures in heaven.

We can be very naïve on this issue. Jesus once told a story about a money manager who was caught embezzling from his master. He went out and cut all sorts of sweetheart debt-reduction deals with his master's borrowers in order to make some friends. Then Jesus makes this application from that surprisingly shady story:

"For the people of this world are more shrewd in dealing with their own kind than are the people of the light" (Luke 16:8 NIV).

At least one thing that means is that worldly-minded people understand the power and potential of money more than the children of light do.

Money has power!

That power is neutral in nature. It can exercise a negative and destructive influence on us, or we can harness it, control it, and get it under God's control, using it to invest in and do great things!

What would happen—what amazing and world-changing things could be done—if Godly, sold-out followers of Christ in the local churches would begin to use their money to invest in eternal things?

Look at the application Jesus made of that parable:

"Whoever can be trusted with very little can also be trusted with much, and whoever is dishonest with very little will also be dishonest with much. So if you have not been trustworthy in handling worldly wealth, who will trust you with true riches? And if you have not been trustworthy with someone else's property, who will give you property of your own?" (Luke 16:10-12 NIV).

God is sizing you up for what you can be trusted with, by how you use what He has given you already.

If we do not begin to understand the importance of this, we will not "store up treasures in heaven."

We will live our whole lives like pagan consumers, spending every dime we make and driven by greed and anxiety. Then, when we die, God will look at us and say something like, "I gave you a career and you made $35,000 or $45,000 a year for forty years. What did you do with that money that bore fruit—that established My purposes?"

Diagnosing Our Relationship with Money

Therefore I tell you, do not worry about your life, what you will eat or drink; or about your body, what you will wear. Is not life more than food, and the body more than clothes?

Look at the birds of the air; they do not sow or reap or store away in barns, and yet your heavenly Father feeds them. Are you not much more valuable than they? Can any one of you by worrying add a single hour to your life? **(Matthew 6:25-27 NIV)**

All of us will say that Jesus has our heart, but what we say is not the test. There are two tests of greed. There are two manifestations of the disease.

Warning 1: Hoarding

Do you find yourself excessively worrying over money? Do you hoard your money? Do you spend your whole life asking yourself questions like "What if I get sick? What if I want to retire before I'm sixty-five? What if something goes bad in the economy? What if I can't take the dream vacation I've always wanted?"

I'm not talking about prudent planning. We all need to do that. I'm talking about an obsessive fear centered around money—whether you have a little or a lot. There are Christians in this world who have more money than they'll ever need, yet they're living in fear that they'll run out and have to live on dog food.

The Lord has blessed them abundantly, but fear makes them hoard just when they could be the greatest blessing to God's kingdom.

Where is the first place you cut in your budget when times get tight? If it's tithing, you have a heart problem.

What percentage of your income do you give away to help others? If it is less than ten percent, you have a heart problem.

Remember, where your treasure and your trust are, that's where your heart is also.

Warning 2: Consumerism

"Consumerism" means that everything that comes your way, you consume. All the dollars that come in become things for you to own. You just consume, consume, consume.

If you just consume as if your life depends on it, then essentially you consume everything, including your own future with consumer debt.

Now, here are the problems with being a consumer or a hoarder. Both are very self-centered. Both leave you living as if there is no God. Both are fueled by the same thing—greed.

Greed is simply the assumption that it's all for your consumption. That's all it is.

You can be poor and greedy; you can be rich and greedy.

Greed is simply the idea that if anything comes to you, it's for you. It's for your consumption. If you live to consume it all now, you are a consumer. If you live to consume it later, you are a hoarder.

Where else but in America would we have measurements of a society like the consumer index and consumer confidence? That is an American, worldly economic measurement. In the kingdom, we should have a giver index and giver confidence!

So what are we going to do about it? What are some practical measures to guard our hearts against the dangers of money? How can we use money in a way that is a huge blessing to God, the church, and the world?

Here are three simple habits to glorify God in the area of money.

1. Give.

What should you do when you get your paycheck? Give a percentage away. When you do this, you're telling God, "This abundance came from You, and now I'm going to bless others with it."

The greatest danger that we face is to make an idol out of the gifts God gives to us. You must determine in your mind, "I will not be ruled by the things God has given me." Besides, it doesn't belong to us, anyway. Everything we have—or ever will have—belongs to God.

2. Save.

Determine to save your money. What's the best way to do that? Pay off your debts. But it's not *just* about getting out of debt. It's about reprioritizing how you use your money altogether. Evaluate where your money is going. Could you cut back on personal pleasures in order to bless those who are needy?

3. Live.

Get on a budget that will allow you to live on *less* than you make.

In summary, here is what you must do to glorify God with your money: Give first, save second, and live on the rest. When you put the right things first, the rest will fall into place.

These three habits are very basic, yet so many people shy away from them, mostly due to laziness, selfishness, and pride. But if you rearrange your life according to these key habits, you will begin storing treasures for yourself in heaven.

So, if you're a Christian today, it's time to have a heart-to-heart with God and say, "God, I've made plenty of excuses with my money, and I've ignored a lot of Your truth about it. But now, I want to put Your kingdom first and my kingdom second, because when I stand before You one day, I want to hear You say, 'Well done, good and faithful servant.' So, please give me wisdom to know how to handle my money from now on."

If you faithfully pray this prayer, God will be faithful to help you pay off your debt, reprioritize your budget, and help you in the areas of contentment and generosity.

CHAPTER NINE

The Race Card

Therefore, remember that formerly you who are Gentiles by birth and called "uncircumcised" by those who call themselves "the circumcision" (which is done in the body by human hands)—remember that at the time you were separate from Christ, excluded from citizenship in Israel and foreigners to the covenants of the promise, without hope and without God in the world. But now in Christ Jesus you who once were far away have been brought near by the blood of Christ. For he himself is our peace, who has made the two groups one and has destroyed the barrier, the dividing wall of hostility, by setting aside in his flesh the law with its commands and regulations. His purpose was to create in himself one new humanity out of the two, thus making peace, and in one body to reconcile both of them to God through the cross, by which he put to death their hostility. He came and preached peace to you who were far away and peace to those who were near. For through him we both have access to the Father by one Spirit. Consequently, you are no longer foreigners and strangers, but fellow citizens with God's people and also members of his household, built on the foundation of the apostles and prophets, with Christ Jesus himself as the chief cornerstone. In him the whole building is joined together and rises to become a holy temple in the Lord. And in him you too are being built together to become a

dwelling in which God lives by his Spirit. ***(Ephesians 2:11-***
22 NIV)

Since the end of World War II, 13,000 people have
been killed or wounded by mines that still lay buried
beneath the surface of the nation of Poland. The Vietnam
war ended in 1973. In the forty-plus years since "peace"
was declared in that country, 11,000 people have been
killed or wounded by the explosives that remain.

Wherever there has been war, casualties will occur
long after peace is declared. That is true literally and in
interpersonal conflict.

Because the camp that declares peace is usually the
winner, and whatever the losing party experiences is not
what they would call peace. Feelings of anger and
frustration remain buried and undetonated in our souls.

For instance, some men think the argument they had
with their wife last week is over. But it's not over. They
might take a wrong step tomorrow, and it's all going to
blow up again. Disputes aren't over just because you
declare they are. The damage runs much deeper than
that.

The bombs lay there, buried beneath our politically
correct surface, waiting for another misstep, another trip
up, to set them off again.

This is what happened in the riots in Ferguson and
Baltimore this last year. It was also in the anger you felt
when you watched news about them on FOX or CNN
(depending on which version of the news you think is
telling the truth and which you believe is lying); and,

whether you are black or white, those images bring very strong emotions to the surface of your soul.

We all decide which version of the narrative we think we believe, take our sides, and then hurl verbal grenades at one another through Facebook and Twitter.

These wounds and this anger are the result of lethal leftovers of past brutality, racism, and the misguided remedies applied by a paternalistic government.

These emotions are buried in every one of our hearts. Ferguson isn't far from wherever you live. But the good news is, where you live isn't that far from Ephesus.

A Human Problem, A Heavenly Plan

It might shock you to realize that racial reconciliation is one of the central themes of the New Testament and one of the main outcomes we are supposed to experience as a result of the cross, the Resurrection, and the active grace of Jesus in our hearts.

Paul writes to the church, *"Therefore, remember"* (Ephesians 2:11 NIV).

He has just finished teaching us again the truth of God's powerful salvation work in our lives in Ephesians 2:1-10.

"Now," he writes, "I want to remind you Jews and Gentiles that one of the effects of that grace is it empowers you to not only be reconciled to God, but to actually be reconciled to one another."

God's grace isn't just about getting you to heaven when you die. It is supposed to make such a change in us so we can actually love one another regardless of our race or cultural background. Dr. Samuel Hines, pastor of Third Street Church of God in Washington D.C., used to say it this way: "Reconciliation is God's one-item agenda."

But race has always been a problem.

First-century Christians didn't walk around with color-blind halos over their eyes. They might have been saved, loved Jesus, and been full of the Holy Spirit, but Jews didn't trust Gentiles and Gentiles didn't like Jews.

However, in this new nation of people called "Christians," the apostles were teaching them, "If you all really love Jesus and really want to honor your God, you aren't allowed to segregate. You aren't allowed to 'ghettoize' the gospel!"

Still, Dr. Martin Luther King, Jr. was absolutely right when he pointed out that Sunday mornings remain our most segregated hour. Why?

We Aren't Honest About Race

Paul does something shocking. He writes, *"Therefore, remember that formerly you who are Gentiles by birth and called 'uncircumcised' by those who call themselves, 'the circumcision'..."* (Ephesians 2:11 NIV).

I have a friend who reminds me, "There is a way black people talk about white people and white people talk about black people when 'it's just us.'" But nobody admits it!

When we are together, we share our "deep concerns" about the societal imbalance that exists between "Caucasians" and "African-Americans." We are so politically correct that we cannot get anything else correct.

Paul just says it! "Hey, look, you all know how we talk about you and we know how you talk about us, but we are in the church now, and we ought to be able to talk to one another."

That type of honesty can clear the ground and get us past being fake with one another so that we can reflect on how God can help us with our sins and shortcomings. Of course, there is another problem. When we do decide to talk, we do it so badly.

"Uncircumcised" was the Jewish racial slur for the Gentiles. And the Gentiles had their names for the Jews. Just like we have names for one another. They are the tags we hang on one another to give ourselves an excuse for not dealing with one another.

If a Jewish believer didn't like the diet or the religious practice of a Gentile, he didn't have to try to understand that person. He just said, "Ah, he is uncircumcised, you know how all those uncircumcised Gentiles are." When a Gentile heard, "They don't eat bacon!" he didn't feel the need to try and understand the contours of that conviction in a Jewish heart. He could just laugh and say, "Well, those Jews, they are all like that, you know."

And this shallow, lazy, hateful approach does the work of erecting barriers.

Paul writes about *"the barrier, the dividing wall of hostility"* (Ephesians 2:14 NIV). He had the barriers and dividing walls that were in the temple in mind. There was a court for all God-fearers, both Jews and Gentiles, then a barrier beyond which only Jews could go, and then a barrier beyond which only Jewish males could go.

We have had barriers like that.

We have placed signs up that said, "This restroom is for Whites only." We drew lines in bus aisles so that people of color knew which seats they could sit in. There were school doors that were closed and opportunities that were shut off.

And we are tempted to mutter impatiently, "That was decades ago; it is time to move on." But pay attention. Paul wrote about a *"dividing wall of hostility."*

When you build a society or grow up in a world with those barriers, an emotion begins to take root—a spirit begins to develop. An invisible barrier rises in human hearts, reinforced by pride, privilege, anger, resentment, and bitterness. A cold, distrustful hostility settles in that continues to divide us long after the physical walls come down. You may not be able to see it, but just try to break through it and you will know that it is real!

Haven't you felt it? Ask yourself why it is so hard for you to talk honestly with someone whose race is different. You just know there things you cannot say and feelings you cannot share—even if you both love Jesus!

So there is the problem. It is deep, and it is entrenched by years of hurt and hostility.

So, How Does God Deal with This?

But now... **(Ephesians 2:13 NIV)**

Those words mean that something has changed. Something is radically different. That was then; this is now!

Paul is writing about the church. And he says that God's purpose in the church is *"to create in himself one new humanity out of the two, thus making peace"* (Ephesians 2:15 NIV). Something is supposed to be happening in the church that the world has never seen before: *"one new humanity..."*

God is not out to make us better White people or better Black people or new and improved Hispanic people. *He is out to make us totally new creations in Christ Jesus!* God is making a new humanity. He is making one new race of us! A race of people who talk, walk, laugh, love, serve, share, and raise our kids differently than any race that has ever existed before!

And someday we will look and see what God sees: *"A great multitude that no one could count, from every nation, tribe, people and language, standing before the throne and before the Lamb....Wearing white robes and...holding palm branches in their hands. And they cried out in a loud voice: 'Salvation belongs to our God, who sits on the throne, and to the Lamb'"* (Revelation 7:9-10 NIV).

And when people look at us and ask, "Who are these people?"

No one will say, "These are the Black Christians or the White Christians or the Hispanic Christians."

No, the answer will be:

"These are they who have come through great tribulation; they have washed their robes and made them white in the blood of the Lamb!"

And Paul shows us how God is doing it:

"But now in Christ Jesus…brought near by the blood of Christ.…He himself is our peace, who has…destroyed the barrier…through the cross, by which he put to death their hostility.…For through him we both have access to the Father by one Spirit" (Ephesians 2:13-18 NIV).

The work of Christ, the gospel, is the power of God not just for our salvation, but also for our reconciliation!

It is critical that we embrace that because the solution has to be radical. Paul says God *"destroyed the barrier"* (verse 14) and *"put to death our hostility"* (verse 16).

That is how you deal with racism! You cannot reason with, educate, or legislate your way around fear and hatred.

I understand what Dr. King meant when he said, "It may be true that the law cannot make a man love me, but it can keep him from lynching me."

But, God has a better plan and a greater power for his people. Jesus did not come to restrain our wickedness or to retrain our evil to be more sensitive. He came to destroy the works of the devil, to take everything that stood against us, even what was in our own hearts, and nail that to his cross!

The solution also has to be personal. After writing about what Jesus did on the cross, Paul writes, *"He came and preached peace…"* (Ephesians 2:17 NIV).

That means after the cross, the living Christ, through the Holy Spirit, has to teach us, preach to us what that sacrifice and shed blood was supposed to mean—what difference it is supposed to make in our lives!

Jesus preaches to us that that cross was about peace. Peace with God but also with one another—they go together. It takes you hearing it directly from Jesus to get that.

That is why so many people who say they believe in and love Jesus still hate one another. They have heard preachers preach about how Jesus died to reconcile them to God, but they have never heard anyone preach that He also died to reconcile them to a Black person or a White person!

If you wonder if that is true, remember the Apostle Peter standing in the home of a bunch of "Gentiles" in Acts 10 and saying, *"I now realize how true it is that God does not show favoritism but accepts from every nation the one who fears him and does what is right"* (Acts 10:34-35 NIV).

Peter had walked with Jesus for three years; he had witnessed the crucifixion and resurrection. He had been a part of the outpouring of the Holy Spirit on Pentecost. But he was still a racist!

But when the resurrected Jesus started preaching to him and the voice of God said, *"What I have called clean, don't you call unclean,"* then Peter understood!

Still, even though it is a miracle…

We Have to Remain Dedicated to the Process

Consequently, you are no longer foreigners and strangers, but fellow citizens with God's people…In him the whole building is joined together and rises to become a holy temple to the Lord. And in him you too are being built together to become a dwelling in which God lives by his Spirit. **(Ephesians 2:19-22 NIV)**

We have to be *"joined together"* and *"built together."* Remember that the church is a temple. They didn't build temples like we build buildings today. Today we start with blocks, not stones.

Blocks are easier. They are all the same size, the same shape, the same weight, and the same color—dull gray.

It is so much easier to build a church with such homogeneity. It is less challenging, there are fewer misunderstandings, and it is less stressful. It is also less miraculous and less God-honoring.

God is not a block-layer; He is a stonemason. He takes living "stones" of all different shapes, sizes, weights, colors, races, and cultures, and He works on them, chisels them, shapes them, and puts them together for Himself.

This process of sanctification—of being shaped and chiseled by God and through the interaction of the saints—hurts. It is uncomfortable. It constantly exposes us to ourselves and to one another.

We would rather be in places where everyone looks like us, worships like us, and votes like us. But God won't have a dull, gray, block temple; He is building a masterpiece of living stones that have learned to relate to one another.

So What Can We Do?

We can try to be honest with ourselves and God.

Ask for His help in not taking on the resentment and hatred and lack of forgiveness we see around this issue in our world.

Ask God if He will help us to start having some honest conversations with one another based upon Scripture and not on political, racial, or cultural prejudices.

We can intentionally try to build friendships with people of other races.

If we have any shot at legitimate racial reconciliation, it cannot be driven by White guilt. It cannot be driven by the need to feel like we need to rescue or pay back. It must be built upon, pushed forward, by the gospel of Jesus Christ.

We are going to have to depend on the Holy Spirit that dwells in us. He does not dwell in the government or any secular civil rights organization. He dwells in the church. That is why the church is the only place where this can possibly happen.

CHAPTER TEN

Gay Marriage

Some Pharisees came to him to test him. They asked, "Is it lawful for a man to divorce his wife for any and every reason?"

"Haven't you read," he replied, "that at the beginning the Creator 'made them male and female,' and said, 'For this reason a man will leave his father and mother and be united to his wife, and the two will become one flesh'? So they are no longer two, but one flesh. Therefore what God has joined together, let no one separate."

"Why then," they asked, "did Moses command that a man give his wife a certificate of divorce and send her away?"

Jesus replied, "Moses permitted you to divorce your wives because your hearts were hard. But it was not this way from the beginning. I tell you that anyone who divorces his wife, except for sexual immorality, and marries another woman commits adultery."

The disciples said to him, "If this is the situation between a husband and wife, it is better not to marry."

Jesus replied, "Not everyone can accept this word, but only those to whom it has been given. For there are eunuchs who were born that way, and there are eunuchs who have been made eunuchs by others—and there are those who

*choose to live like eunuchs for the sake of the kingdom of
heaven. The one who can accept this should accept it."*
(Matthew 19:3-12 NIV)

They asked about marriage.

The Pharisees were debating what was permissible in
regard to marriage and divorce. Now Jesus had come to
their area so they asked him.

People are still debating very controversial questions
about marriage. If Oprah were doing the interview, the
question would most likely be, "Is it lawful for a man to
marry another man, or a woman to marry another
woman?" It is a different question, but it involves the
same issue—the nature of marriage and what is
permissible in God's eyes. Thankfully, they were asking
Jesus and not the United States Supreme Court.

Some in our culture don't care what God thinks at all
on the topic. However, there is a relentless segment that
tries to get the divine stamp of approval on any approach
they want to take to marriage.

They, like these Pharisees, try to appeal to Scripture
and are increasingly hostile toward the established truths
of the church concerning marriage. They are hostile not
because they have proven that those teachings are wrong
or untrue, but because they have decided it is evil,
unloving, unchristian, or just outdated to oppose any gay
preference or practice.

Wannabe sophisticates and societal trailblazers hurl
arguments at orthodoxy like, "Even if you think this is a
'sin,' why do you harp on it so much?" They opine,
"There are so many other worse sins, like sex trafficking

and racism. You seem to be fixated on homosexuality to an unfair degree."

This shouting down does much to aid the cause of those who favor gay marriage. The response to these arguments is fairly straightforward.

"Sin" Is "Sin"

We do not get to ignore some sins just because others are worse. In the end, I am not certain that we can legitimately make those judgments. The Scriptures pretty much treat sin as a seamless garment. James tells us that if we offend at any point we are guilty of it all.

But the bigger issue is, we have to speak out against this particular sin because this is the one that people are trying to justify today. Jesus wasn't fixated on divorce! Jesus spoke the way He did because men divorcing their wives for *"any and every reason"* was the abuse of God's law that people of the day were trying to justify. That is why we have to speak as directly and often as we do today about gay marriage.

Of course, there is an even bigger reason. Did you notice that these Pharisees were debating the rights of men in marriage? Not one word is spoken, or thought given, about the price the women paid when the men exercised their culturally granted marital rights in a selfish, godless, and sinful way.

When the only determining factor of what we should do and shouldn't do is the assertion, "It is my right," we will behave destructively. Other people will pay a price. When it comes to gay marriage, if we insist on individual rights being the only consideration, then the outcome will be, and is, diseased and destructive for our society as a whole.

So when they asked, "Does the man have the right to divorce his wife?" Jesus doesn't talk about the man's rights. He teaches them what *is* right. What is true and good for us all. That is the approach we need to take on the issue of gay marriage as well.

Thinking Biblically

Jesus's response to the question is to ask a penetrating question of his own: *"Haven't you read...?"*

We don't ask, "What do you prefer?" or, "What does the law make allowances for?" Or, "What did the Supreme Court of the United States rule?"

We ask, "What have we read in the Scriptures?" That seems obvious, I could walk into a lot of churches and begin a series of questions on important issues in that same way. Like:

"Haven't you read what the Scriptures say about divorce?" Or "Haven't you read what the Scriptures say about shacking up with a person you are not married to?" And you would be amazed at the absolute lack of scriptural framework people have for their thoughts and decisions concerning any relationship—including marriage. Just like the Pharisees, we take our cues from many places other than Scripture.

Jesus quotes Genesis 1:27 and 2:24. These verses confront us with these Biblical facts. Marriage is not a cultural institution; rather, it is a divine creation. It is no mistake that Jesus refers to his Father as *"the Creator"* in this passage.

Just like God created the earth, the sea, the stars, and the animals, he created marriage. When it comes to marriage, he created *"male and female."* Finally, the scripture Jesus quotes says, *"For this reason..."*

God designed everything about marriage for a reason. God had a reason that both "male and female" were necessary to make a marriage. This creation and intention predates any law or constitution or act of Congress. Marriage is a spiritual reality, not a legal one.

We have been secularized into seeing marriage as just two people who are fond of one another, exchanging rings, and having approved sex. So we ask, "Why can't gay people do that?" Being affectionate toward each other, having sex, wearing matching rings, and even having a state-issued license doesn't equal marriage. Society doesn't get to define marriage; the creator of marriage did that.

So, Christ-followers can't accept gay marriage. Not because we're homophobic, intolerant, or unloving, but because we trust the wisdom of God and recognize His sovereignty, even over the ways we relate to one another—especially in marriage.

The scriptures Jesus cites make it clear that the purpose God had for marriage was covenant unity developed and deepened by sexual intimacy, the creation and nurturing of families, and reflecting the image of God as *"male and female."* So, His response to the divorce question also addresses our questions about gay marriage.

Gay marriage represents a denial of the two-fold nature of man as male and female. Gays and lesbians cannot become one flesh, cannot be fruitful and multiply, cannot adequately reflect the fullness of the image of God, and cannot discharge their sexual drives in a manner consistent with God's Word.

The fact is, people who believe the Scriptures know this: "gay marriage" is not marriage. It is a nonsensical term. The concept is a fabrication of a corrupt society.

Resisting Compromise

The Pharisees respond to Jesus' clear, and I am sure infuriating, teaching by trotting out Moses. We see this tactic used often by those in the religious-minded community who wish to gain approval for perversion of marriage.

They will trot out the "Old Testament versus the New Testament" arguments. They will try to pit Jesus against Moses, or Jesus against Paul, or simply try to ignore the authority of some portions of Scripture altogether. You have heard all the arguments and justifications.

1. **"Well, Jesus never said anything about gay marriage being wrong."**

Of course, that is a weak "argument from silence." Jesus never said anything about polygamy or pedophilia or a dozen other perversions we could mention. However, we seem to have enough moral sense and he seemed to believe our Creator had given us enough intelligence to know that those things did not fall in line with His creation-intent when He designed marriage.

2. "Well, the New Testament speaks differently than the Old on a lot of human rights issues."

There is a progressive revelation of God's will when it comes to slavery, women's rights, etc. The same is true when it comes to homosexuality and gay marriage.

The rebuttal to that is found in the statement itself. Yes, those issues are spoken of differently as revelation progressed. However, homosexuality is condemned in both testaments.

Also, Jesus himself, when asked about marriage, references the Old Testament creation narrative and affirms its unchanging nature. One man with one woman for a lifetime was, and remains, the definition of marriage. Any adjustment, including the mosaic concession to divorce and the modern perversion of gay marriage represents a regression, not progress, in revelation.

Then there is the classic:

3. "They are born gay, and so they cannot help it. It is unloving and unchristian for us to ask them not to pursue their natural inclinations."

Well, the immediate rebuttal at hand is simply that this is a lie. There is absolutely no objective evidence anywhere that proves that people are born genetically predisposed to be gay. But there is a second reason why this argument cannot sway us.

Predisposition to a certain sin does not equal predetermination or justification for that sin.

Married men are sometimes attracted to multiple women who are not their wives. Does this mean they should self-identify as polygamists? And surely you wouldn't consider it hateful for Christians to encourage married men *not* to act on their desires in an effort to remain faithful to their spouses.

All people are born with a predisposition toward some sin. Some people are inclined more than others to lie, some to steal, some to anger, some to drunkenness. Some people may have an inclination to heterosexual promiscuity while some will struggle with homosexual desire. The real issue is not what you desire to do, but what God says is right or wrong.

Just because someone likes the taste of beer more than someone else doesn't mean he gets a pass on being a drunk. That's sin. And just because someone may have a homosexual desire doesn't mean he gets a pass on acting out on that desire. That's sin.

We know sin of all sorts is both a predisposition and a learned behavior, but we still tell people not to commit sins because it is destructive to them and it is detrimental to those around them and to society.

Unflinching Challenge

Well, of course, when such truth is spoken so plainly it gets a reaction—even from Jesus disciples! They get all bug-eyed and essentially say, "Jesus, if that is what God demands from us in marriage, if that is how it has to be, it may be better for people not to marry."

That seems drastic, but notice that Jesus doesn't deny it. He basically responds by saying, "For some people that is exactly the option they need to take. That is the choice they need to make."

What we have forgotten, but Jesus never did, was that marriage is God's creation and God takes it very seriously. Marriage isn't a relationship you enter into just because you want to or because you have a right to do it. Marriage is a sacred commitment you make to another person, and to God. Marriage is a promise to conduct yourself toward that other person and before God in a certain, selfless way—for life. In sickness and health, for richer or poorer, through good times and bad, babies and bottles, battles and bills.

There is no cheap way in, and there should be no easy way out. It is the most demanding, and the most rewarding relationship humans are offered the opportunity to be a part of. And it is God who created and sanctified the relationship. One man and one woman doing life that way together until they are parted by death. No alternatives are given.

If you look at that and think, "I don't think I can do that," or, "I don't want to do marriage that way," then don't.

If we cannot live that standard, we should at least stop trying to lower it.

CHAPTER ELEVEN

Politics

Keeping a close watch on him, they sent spies, who pretended to be sincere. They hoped to catch Jesus in something he said, so that they might hand him over to the power and authority of the governor. So the spies questioned him: "Teacher, we know that you speak and teach what is right, and that you do not show partiality but teach the way of God in accordance with the truth. Is it right for us to pay taxes to Caesar or not?"

He saw through their duplicity and said to them, "Show me a denarius. Whose image and inscription are on it?"

"Caesar's," they replied.

He said to them, "Then give back to Caesar what is Caesar's, and to God what is God's." **(Luke 20:20-25 NIV)**

Preachers get into trouble talking about politics.

Getting Jesus into trouble was exactly what these men were trying to do when they approached him with a question about taxes.

Thankfully, Jesus knew he had nothing to fear and he knew what was true even when it came to politics. Because of that, we have his answer to learn from.

Still, the whole interaction does make a few things crystal clear:

Politics haven't changed much. When it comes to political matters, sincerity is rare. Luke tells us that these men *"pretended to be sincere."* Well that just about describes every politician!

Politics makes you very good at pretending to be sincere, pretending to want honest discussions, pretending to want real solutions that benefit all the people. Whether it is healthcare or employment or your taxes, politicians pretend to be honest. They have to, because of this next fact about politics:

There is always a hidden agenda. These men didn't ask questions of Jesus and listen to his answer so they could learn about Him, God, or government. They were listening so they could *"catch Jesus in something he said"* and ruin Him. They were looking for a sound bite to use in a smear campaign.

Two chapters later, when Jesus is standing in front of the governor, they began to accuse Him, saying, *"We have found this man subverting our nation. He opposes payment of taxes to Caesar and claims to be Messiah, a king"* (Luke 23:2 NIV).

Did Jesus tell them not to pay taxes to Caesar? Absolutely not. But what someone *really* said matters very little when you have a hidden agenda.

Politics are always about expediency.

Scholars say there were two groups that were questioning Jesus: the Herodians and the Pharisees.

Now, the Herodians tended to go along with whoever was in control. The Pharisees, on the other hand, believed in standing behind their principles, so they resisted the government whenever it clashed with their beliefs. Yet, these two groups formed an alliance to sabotage Jesus. It would be like Rush Limbaugh and Jesse Jackson working together.

When it comes to politics, principle will often be set aside for expediency. So, since these are consistent characteristics of any political issue for all time periods, let me make one observation:

Nobody owns Jesus. The hot-button political issue in Palestine that year: taxes. (Again I ask, has anything really changed?) And, at the risk of sounding like a simple hick of a preacher, let me tell you why: selfishness.

When it comes to taxes, what we are arguing about is "How much will you take from me?" on one hand, and "How much will you give to me?" on the other. That is what that issue is about! Me! It always is!

But whether it is taxes, gay rights, abortion, or illegal immigration, what people were trying to do with Jesus and religion then, they still try to do today. They are trying to own Jesus.

They are trying to get him to endorse their candidates or justify their agenda.

Jesus responds in a masterful way. They really should have anticipated this. They asked Him to show them what was right. That word comes from the Greek root *ortho*. It means "straight." It is where we get our words like "orthodontist" (straight teeth).

So they said, "Master, we know you will not play games, you will give it to us straight."

Jesus did.

He started by showing them, and us:

The Legitimate Role of Government

He saw through their duplicity and said to them, "Show me a denarius. Whose image and inscription are on it?"

"Caesar's," they replied.

He said to them, "Then give back to Caesar what is Caesar's, and to God what is God's." (Luke 20:23-25 NIV)

Why did Jesus ask for a specific coin? Two reasons:

1. Symbolism

Every coin has two sides, so what Jesus was illustrating was that we, as Christian citizens, are simultaneously living in two worlds.

Yes, we are citizens of our country here on earth, but Scripture tells us *"...our citizenship is in heaven"* (Philippians 3:20 NIV). So we have a responsibility to balance our dual citizenship, obligations to our God and to our government, and we need to think very clearly about how those two relate to one another.

2. Tangible evidence

Jesus asked for a denarius to show to these men— especially the ones who thought that the government didn't have any rights in their lives—that it actually did have a legitimate role to play in their lives.

When I was young, if you wanted to play video games—I mean the really cool video games—you had to go to an arcade. If you went to the arcade there was only one coin that would work: a quarter.

In the same way, if you were going to pay your poll taxes, there was only one coin you could use, and that was the denarius. These men were posing as rebels, but when Jesus asked for a tax coin, they had it on hand.

His point was: "You're saying you want to lead a tax rebellion, but you're carrying around tax coins in your purse. If you're trading with Caesar's coin, if you're driving on Caesar's roads, if you're protected by Caesar's army, then you owe Caesar something. So pay him what you owe him."

In Romans 13:1, Paul says, *"Let everyone be subject to the governing authorities, for there is no authority except that which God has established"* (NIV).

So government has a legitimate role to play in our lives. No human government is perfect. And few perfectly represent or enforce God's authority. But I do believe that the United States government was God ordained, and we're blessed to live under this government.

We cannot accept the benefits that our country provides, but neglect our responsibilities as Christian citizens. We are called to render unto Caesar what is Caesar's.

Romans 13:6-7 says, *"This is also why you pay taxes, for the authorities are God's servants, who give their full time to governing. Give to everyone what you owe them: If you owe taxes, pay taxes"* (NIV).

Paul sounds like a crazy Democrat, doesn't he? But although Jesus makes it clear that human government has a legitimate role in our lives, He also makes this clear:

The Limited Role of Government

The very same God who ordained government also sets limits on it. Let me highlight a couple:

Human governments have limited power. There are some puzzles that no government can solve. There are some problems no government can fix. There are some things that only God can do. Here's the crazy thing: There were people in the crowd that day who really thought that if they got the right government in place, the world would be okay. There were people who believed that if Jesus would help them get this tax issue fixed and help them overthrow the oppression of Rome and install a new king, then everything would be dandy in the world.

There are still people who think that if you elect the right president, if you elect the right senator, if you could just get the democrats or the republicans out of the White House, then Utopia would finally come.

Government can lower our taxes, but they can't raise our kids. They can't pay our bills. They can't enforce morality or tolerance. Government cannot make everyone love baseball, hot dogs, apple pie, and speak English while they're doing it.

Even if all your favorite candidates got elected, and all your propositions got passed, this world would still be a desperate, dark place. Can the government restore real love to your marriage? Can the government make husbands and wives love and respect each other?

Can the government stop corporate leaders in America from finding new ways to steal? Does the government have the power to make us sexually moral or honest or self-sacrificial? These things do not reside in the realm of our government. The Kingdom of God will never be ushered in by any human system, because no human system can touch the human heart.

Luke 17:20-21 says, *"Being asked by the Pharisees when the kingdom of God would come, Jesus replied, 'The coming of the kingdom of God is not something that can be observed, nor will people say, "Here it is," or "There it is," because the kingdom of God is in your midst'"* (NIV).

Human governments have limited authority in our lives. Jesus says to *"give back to Caesar what is Caesar's, and to God what is God's"* (NIV).

This is more radical and revolutionary than we understand. Rome insisted that Caesar was God. So since Caesar was supposedly God, he had a right to every aspect in their lives. And although Jesus makes it very clear that Caesar has some legitimate authority over us, there are some areas only God has authority.

In the book of Acts, there is an account of Peter and John healing a lame man outside the gate of the temple. This caused a big ruckus. When Peter sees the curious crowd gathering, he preaches a message, and thousands of people come to faith.

However, the disciples are arrested and dragged before the Sanhedrin. That governing body tells them to stop preaching in the name of Jesus.

Peter replied, *"We must obey God rather than men"* (ESV).

By saying this, Peter was setting a limit on governmental authority.

Human governments are limited because they are human. Only God is God. That truth is what led Christians like William Wilberforce to stand up against slavery in England. It is what led Christians like Dietrich Bonheoffer to stand up against the Nazi party during World War II.

It is what led Christian men like Martin Luther King, Jr., to resist Caesar. When any law violates what is written in God's Word, Christians have a responsibility to reject it and resist it.

The Responsibility of Believers

As representatives of Jesus Christ, we're told that in order to resist being conformed to this present world, we have to be transformed by the renewing of our minds. In short, we have to change the way we think.

We are responsible for immersing our minds in God's truth so that our ethics, our morals, and our political views are kept in line with God's truth.

When these guys came to Jesus, they had one agenda on their mind: taxes. They wanted to know if Jesus was on their side or Caesar's side. But as Christ followers, we cannot think so narrowly or selfishly.

Jesus said we were to render unto Caesar, and that seems to indicate that we have to be involved with Caesar. So, whether we're angry, tired, or disillusioned, we are not allowed to withdraw and become a cynic. Cynicism is the chief retreat of a lazy soul. You're called to exert influence in this world.

Honoring God in Politics

1. Pray for your leaders.

I urge, then, first of all, that petitions, prayers, intercession and thanksgiving be made for all people—for kings and all those in authority, that we may live peaceful and quiet lives in all godliness and holiness. This is good, and pleases God

*our Savior, who wants all people to be saved and to come
to a knowledge of the truth.* **(1 Timothy 2:1-4 NIV)**

Pray that God will help our authorities to govern in a
way that creates a culture where we will be allowed to
live a holy life in peace and not persecution. Pray that
they will create an environment where more and more
people can hear the gospel and be saved.

How's that for a political agenda? What would
happen if we started praying like that? What would
happen if churches really began to conduct prayer
meetings for our government?

2. Vote.

One time, D. L. Moody, one of the great Christian
evangelists, was walking down the street in Chicago, and
a pastor friend stopped him and asked, "Where are you
going, Pastor Moody?" And Moody said, "I'm going to
go vote."

And the guy said, "Mr. Moody, don't you know that
your citizenship is in heaven?" And Moody said, "Yes,
but I own property in Cook County."

If you're a part of this country, you ought to be
voting. Martin Luther King, Jr. said, "The law cannot
make a man love me, but it can keep him from lynching
me."

People who love their country and want to see it
create an atmosphere that we pray for ought to vote.
That's how you exert influence as a Christian citizen.

3. Serve your city.

We have to take personal responsibility for our city. No government, no politician, no president, no political action group is our hope. So, while we can pray for our leaders and vote for the people who make the laws, don't let politics be a cop-out for your personal responsibility. You are a citizen of the United States.

The church is the solution. You and I are the solution. We have the power, through Christ, to change the world. So, stop ignoring problems and start exerting influence by serving your city in the name of Jesus. Just ask God what He would have you do to make a difference.

4. Be cautious.

Jesus asked, "Whose image and inscription are on this coin?"

That word "image" was loaded with meaning for his Jewish audience. As soon as they heard it they would think of the verse in Genesis, *"So God created mankind in his own image, in the image of God he created them; male and female he created them"* (Genesis 1:26-27 NIV).

In holding that coin and asking that question, Jesus is reminding us, "Caesar made the coin, so if he wants to put his image on your money, then fine. But who made you? Who created you? Who stamped his image on your heart?"

So if Caesar's image is on your coin, give it to him, but God's image is on your heart and soul. Only God deserves your full, undivided allegiance of heart and soul.

Make sure the lines in your heart stay clear. Never give Caesar what belongs to God. Never let your faith became the tool of any political party. I'm longing for the day when preachers stop inviting politicians to speak to their congregations. Stop equating your political party with the Word of God. The real need for this world is still for Jesus and for the church.

And so we read, we debate, we pray, we love, and we serve—all in the confidence that we're still waiting for the true King to come back.

About The Author

Jack Hilligoss is a husband, father, pastor, and Christ follower. He has been a pastor for 27 years, discipling and equipping believers from small churches in Midwestern cornfields to multi-cultural churches in the inner city, to a growing and community-impacting church in Lake Wales, Florida. During that time, he has learned that people are all very much the same. They have the same questions and they need the same hope. And, he has learned, everyone needs a pastor—someone who will help them think about life; someone who will show them how to hold their lives up to the light of Scripture and see from a perspective that may give them eternal meaning in the midst of the temporal rush of life. That is Jack's passion, and that is how he has spent his life.

About Sermon To Book

SermonToBook.com began with a simple belief: that sermons should be touching lives, *not* collecting dust. That's why we turn sermons into high-quality books that are accessible to people all over the globe.

Turning your sermon series into a book exposes more people to God's Word, better equips you for counseling, accelerates future sermon prep, adds credibility to your ministry, and even helps make ends meet during tight times.

John 21:25 tells us that the world itself couldn't contain the books that would be written about the work of Jesus Christ. Our mission is to try anyway. Because, in Heaven, there will no longer be a need for sermons or books. Our time is now.

If God so leads you, we'd love to work with you on your sermon or sermon series.

Visit www.sermontobook.com to learn more.

Encourage the Author by Reviewing This Book

If you've found this book helpful or challenging, the author would love your honest feedback. Please consider stopping by Amazon.com and writing a review.

To submit a review, simply go to *Untouchables*' Amazon.com page, click "Write a customer review" in the Customer Reviews section, and click submit.

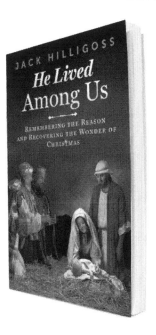

COMING CHRISTMAS 2015

Learn more at jackhilligoss.com

Christmas is a strange and powerful season.

Most of us have wrapped it up in lights and tinsel and buried it under stories of elves, flying reindeer, and a fat man in a red suit. Then we left it in our closet of childhood memories to dust off each December as an escape from "real life."

But Christmas is not an escape or a fantasy. Christmas happened in "real life."

At Christmas, God lived among us—and He showed us how to live by living. It's time for us to follow His example!

Made in the USA
San Bernardino, CA
23 October 2015